Wisdom From Others

9 Life Lessons From My Dad

Donita M. Brown

DARR, LLC

SPRINGFIELD, TN

DARR
3847 Cage Ellis Road
Springfield, TN 37172
www.donitabrown.com

Book Layout © 2017 BookDesignTemplates.com

Wisdom From Others – 9 Life Lessons From My Dad/ Donita M. Brown. -- 1st ed.
ISBN 978-1721223497

Dedicated to my family.

There is wisdom all around us; we only need to listen to hear it.

Contents

CHAPTER 1

Introduction

"There is a wisdom of the head, and a wisdom of the heart."
- Charles Dickens

A PARENT`S LOVE is difficult to explain. It's hard to understand how you can love another person so much. It's different from romantic love. Honestly, I'm not sure I really understood parental love until I became a parent - even though I have parents who loved me dearly.

Understanding the "why" behind that love is a challenge and awkward to express in words; it really is best to be felt. When my oldest child was born, I felt so vulnerable. I loved her so much; I would do anything to protect her from harm.

I gave my dad, Ken also called Kenneth or Kenny by some, the draft copy of this book as we hiked on a warm December day in the Great Smoky Mountains National Park. He, my sister Danielle, and I had all been training to hike the Cades Cove driving loop.

This hike was a different hike for us – it was paved, which is odd for a hiker to want to conquer, but conquer it we did. We trained and planned for it for several months, as it was eleven miles long. The letter on the next page is how I first told my Dad about this book.

In John 3:16 NKJV, the writer says: "For God so loved the world that He gave His only begotten Son, that whoever believes in Him should not perish but have everlasting life."

We are told that God gave His Son, Jesus Christ, to save the world. I can't imagine how it feels to give your child to save others.

As parents, we give a little bit of ourselves every day to guard our children's hearts and minds. My dad, Kenneth Taylor, did the same thing for my sisters and me; he gave so much of himself. The lessons contained in this book are testaments of his gift to us.

If you are a parent, I want you to know that you are enough. It may not seem that way at times, but you are. I do not know if my Dad knew he was enough for us while my sisters and I were growing up. I'm sure he had questions and doubts about that many times. As I reflect on the contents of these pages and when these stories took place, I realize I never thought about how

Dad was feeling. I did not consider what he was going through at the time.

Parents, I want you to know your children see you as heroes. Today, I can truly say that my Dad, the main character in this book, is a hero. He is my hero.

The stories you are about to read are true and happened as I remember them. Some of the stories occurred many years ago; others are relatively recent as I have shared some of the stories of my own family.

Time heals all wounds, but sometimes, it also clouds reality. It was only a couple of months ago that I understood what my Dad meant when he said: "There will always be someone better than you." But, all the stories are rich in family culture and love.

My Dad, an unassuming guy, raised three daughters. At the age of 20, he married a lady he loved or should I say, thought he loved, and they quickly started a family. Unfortunately, they could not make the marriage work, and they got divorced. Unlike most family stories like this, my Dad was left to be the primary caregiver for my sisters and me in the late 1980s. That was during a time when fathers did not usually have joint custody or full custody. He and my mom co-parented us before those terms were mainstream.

Dad was not a perfect father, but he tried hard to give us a great life, and he succeeded. In his quest to provide an excellent life for us, he imparted profound and candid wisdom that has stuck with me throughout my life. It has provided a roadmap for nearly every decision I have made.

I remember when I was pregnant with my second daughter; I confided in a co-worker who had two children that I was so worried about having a second child because I loved my first child so much. I was concerned that I would not have enough love in my heart for another child. She reassured me that I didn't need to worry, "Your heart will get bigger," she said. Her message was simple: when you have more to love your heart grows; it does not divide.

Love is like wisdom; it grows when there is more of it to share. The more people you love and the more opportunities you have to love, the higher your capacity to love others.

Wisdom also multiplies the more it is lovingly given. My Dad gave my sisters and me both love and wisdom. He fostered those two qualities in us. I am so grateful for his influence in our lives that I am compelled to write this book as a tribute to my Dad while he can still enjoy it, not after he has gone from this world.

There are three parts to this book:

Part I - Wisdom from a grieving parent
Part II - Wisdom from an adventurous parent
Part III - Wisdom from a caring parent

Part I shares an inspiring lesson that there are everyday heroes among us, doing great things, being stronger than you can imagine, and sharing wisdom, always. You just have to listen to find them. My Dad, is an incredible man, he offered no more or less wisdom than anyone else – I only listened. *There is wisdom all around us, we only need to listen to hear it.*

Part II focuses on adventure, the lessons learned from days and nights spent camping, exploring, learning, and discovering.

Part III, the last section, you will see how my Dad graduated from parenting young children to parenting teenagers and adults. Every day, he still shares some wisdom with me, as there is rarely a day that goes by that we don't talk on the phone or in person. I don't always have the ears to hear, but he continues to plant those seeds of knowledge.

My Dad is a caring father, and now, he is a dear friend. Even in my forties, he still lets me know he's still my Dad.

He doesn't have a college education. He has worked for the same company for 40 years; he's an optician, which means he works with his hands and his heart, connecting to people. He's a studier and lover of people.

As you read his words of wisdom, I hope you will be as inspired and blessed as I have. May you reflect and give thought to the wisdom others have shared with you and together, let us start a movement.

So jump to Twitter, Instagram, Facebook and share *Wisdom from Others* with the hashtag #WisdomFromOthers.

Let's make wisdom grow.

CHAPTER 2

Letter To My Dad

"The most important influence in my childhood was my father." - Beau Bridges

DEAR DAD,

I've been working on this book for a long time. This year, I decided for my 40th birthday, I would finish it.

About ten years ago, I started keeping a list of the words of wisdom and the things you said to me; these are the pieces of advice that have shaped me. Yes, the ones I rolled my eyes at when I was in high school – "watch the weather," or "there will always be someone better than you."

Five years ago, in those stolen moments between work, family, and church, I started writing a little bit of the stories.

This year for my 40th birthday, I decided to start working with a book coach. With her help, I have completed the draft, which is on the following pages. Writing this book has been an all-consuming and very therapeutic experience. It's incredible how the wisdom you revealed to me over the years has shaped me as a person and primarily as a parent.

Several times, you mentioned to me that we all have stories. I specifically remember you talking about Little Papaw and wishing that someone would have recorded his stories because they were so colorful. We recently spoke about the waiter at the Mexican restaurant and wondered what his story was. Dad, we all have stories, but yours are extraordinary and should be shared with others.

The following pages contain our stories. Dad, believe it or not, I listened to what you said. It may not have seemed so, but I did. Sometimes, I still roll my eyes at your wisdom, but even at 40, I realize your parental experience is full of insight.

With your permission, after you read this book, I would like to print it and share the wisdom you've so lovingly given me with others.
Dad, you are my hero, my biggest fan, and I want you to know that I am your biggest fan.

I love you,

Donita

DONITA M. BROWN

Part I:
Wisdom from a Grieving Parent

Lesson 1

Cry Later

"Each day of our lives we make deposits in the memory banks of our children." - Charles R. Swindoll

"DAD, YOU CAN CRY TOO," I said, standing barefoot in purple jam shorts and a neon green shirt with my long brown hair in a side ponytail. My style, like many other ten-year-olds of that time, was modeled after the cool Punky Brewster.

My Dad and I were standing in the kitchen of our white farm-style house. Our rambling house was located on 5th Avenue in Springfield, Tennessee. We lived in a middle-to-lower class neighborhood on a busy two-lane highway. This busy road was the main thoroughfare to the local high school, Springfield High School, the home of the Yellow Jackets.

I felt homesick but oddly was at home. This feeling of melancholy made me physically ill; my lips were trembling, my eyes watering, and I had a queasiness in my gut. It felt like this feeling would never go away.

I was missing my mom. This was the first night without her. The first night after she decided it was better to live without us. *Why did life have to change?* I thought to myself. I wondered why we could not just go back to the way it was before she left and wished someone could put the pieces back together. Unfortunately, when a heart is broken, much like glass, it does not mend easily. And my Dad's heart was broken. My heart was broken. Our family was broken.

From that moment on, my sisters and I would forever have a "Mom's house" and a "Dad's house."

My Dad looked at me through his wise brown eyes holding back the tears and motioned for me to come to him. His lips trembled the way I have rarely seen in the many years since. I didn't know if he could hold back the tears stored in his heart. His strong face was scratchy from the day's five o'clock shadow; it looked so sad – as if it could not be healed by anything I could provide. Healing a broken heart takes time.

Dad must have been wondering how to comfort his daughters and worried that he might not say the right things. He hugged me and let me cry. This was a tender moment between father and daughter. My tears were so big and shoulder drenching, they gave me a headache and made my face splotchy. The emotional grieving process exhausted me.

My dad was sitting at our kitchen table. A goldenrod chrome dinette with a leaf that seated six. It had a nice oval shape when there were five of us sitting at it. But after that night, I never remembered that table with the leaf and the six chairs. It was as if the two additional chairs had left and the leaf stored away in a closet, never to be seen again. From that day, the plastic table, if it could talk, would share stories of homework, class projects, serious father-daughter talks, and of course, many meals.

My parents purchased this table when they got married in 1976. They had been married twelve years before Mom left. Like everything else in our house, the kitchen table was nothing fancy. But our white rambling house dotted with black shutters and a sloping backyard with a swing set that my sisters and I spent many hours on, was our home or used to be home with a family of five.

It was 1987. I was ten years old and my sisters, fraternal twins, were five. We had just finished supper, which included canned biscuits that tasted delicious to us then. The biscuits had probably been on sale. They were served with the intent that we (Dad, two sisters and I) would finish everything on the table, no leftovers. Dad did not like leftovers. In all the years, I can never remember ever having leftovers in our house. The canned biscuits were served with Blue Bonnet Butter, fish sticks, and cream corn.

I am not sure why my dad loved cream corn, but he did. Maybe he liked it because it was sweeter than the regular corn. He has always had a sweet tooth, and you had better hide your chocolate when he is nearby because he is a genius at sniffing it out! It's odd for a man to have such a sweet tooth and still stay so lean, especially when we always had margarine in the house and never real butter. Everyone knows that margarine makes you fat. But at the time margarine was cheap and we needed cheap.

From the time of that first meal as a family of four, we would have vegetables with dinner. I do not remember what we ate before my mother left but I vividly remember the meals afterward.

Mealtime was special. It was our time to cook together.

The moments we spent preparing food were peppered with the discussion of the day, the radio playing in the background, and love. There was always love in our house, even after my mom left. It was the one time when chores did not matter; homework was forgotten, and the stresses of the day were gone. We just enjoyed being together while we cooked supper then sat and ate with each other.

My name is Donita, and my sisters are Danielle and Deidre. I'm not sure why my parents named us all with a "D" name, as it was terribly frustrating for them at times. Our names turned out to be tongue twisters, not only for them but for anyone who knew the three of us.

I was named after my grandmother, who gave my mom up for adoption. Why I was named after this lady who did not want the opportunity to know my mom is beyond me; plus, the name has always haunted me. Donita. It has such an odd ring to it. My sisters Danielle and Deidre are much better named.

My grandmother, Donita, was a full-blooded Dakota Sioux, who was said to have been so beautiful, she would stop traffic. At the very young age of eighteen, she met my adventurous, strikingly handsome, and wildly creative chef grandfather, named John Lewis Cox. Everyone called him J. L., and he could cook the most amazing meals. He had magic in his hands because someone could use the same ingredients and not get the results he did. His food was pure art.

Neither Donita nor J. L understood what being a parent or married meant in 1957, the year my mom was born. For a short time, Mom lived with her mother Donita on the Indian Reservation in South Dakota. But Mom's stay was short-lived. At the age of 3, she permanently moved in with J. L.'s parents, the Cox's. They were a fundamental Baptist couple and old before their time. They had already raised two sons before my mom went to live with them.

Donita and J. L.'s story could be written as a movie romance. Young love that was not meant to be.

The only time my father ever lied to me was over a vegetable. It was a regular school night when he had three children to wrangle in from school, prepare dinner, and make sure all the homework was completed.

Hominy.

A vegetable that never graced our table after that night. My dad had bought a can of hominy at the Kroger grocery store on Memorial Boulevard. He was looking for an alternative to our regular cream style sweet corn, peas, green beans, and mixed vegetables (which were always Veg-All) rotation. He thought we would like the white vegetable. Dad often saw Wanda, a friend of his who worked at Kroger. I remember many times when with three children in tow, he would take us to Wanda and leave one or both of my sisters with her. Wanda was a thin, beautiful blond and most importantly, a kind lady. She would let my sisters help her scan the groceries while Dad shopped in peace.

"It tastes like popcorn," Dad told my sisters and me. He said he ate hominy growing up and loved it. I have never forgotten that lie. Hominy then and forever has tasted like gray death. I count myself very fortunate that was the only lie he ever told me.

We always ate canned vegetables; they were never fresh or frozen, and invariably, they were purchased at that Kroger store. We never shopped anywhere else even though there were other grocery stores in town. A tribute, perhaps, to Dad's need to have a routine: something he could control in our chaotic lives and a testament to his loyalty.

Green beans, cream style sweet corn, peas and mixed vegetables – those were our staples. Faithfully, Dad would always rinse the can. He never used the water that came with the canned vegetables when he heated them up as if by rinsing them he could make them healthier. He always opened the cans with the same can opener. We only had one, and he would stand by the kitchen sink, take a deep breath, sigh, drain the vegetables, pour them into a saucepan, fill the pan with water, and heat them up. There was magic in the love he used to prepare the vegetables.

When my parents got a divorce, I was in the 5th grade at Westside Elementary, and my sisters were in kindergarten at Cheatham Park.

Both schools were in Springfield, TN, but not close enough for us to walk to either. Thankfully, my dad had the type of job where he could take us to school or have someone pick us up; we never had to ride the bus. That was a sacrifice he made for us, his three darling daughters.

Dad did not have to take the responsibility of raising three girls. He could have told my mom to take custody of us and be our sole caregiver, but he didn't. Later in life, I realized Dad never saw us as obligations; rather, he felt it was a privilege to be there for us. He remained in our lives not because he had to but because he wanted to.

Springfield, a small town, is thirty miles from everywhere. Depending on the decade, the state of the factories, the city leaders, and their acceptance or rejection of expansion, Springfield is either a booming small town or a sad little show of what could be (with other towns booming nearby), often held back by limited thinking.

I never saw my parents fight before they got divorced. Not once! And so, I was shocked when my mom who was then in her thirties, sat me down in my sisters' room with two twin beds and told me that she was going to live somewhere else. "You probably figured it out," she said. I was dumbfounded; for at the age of ten, I had not guessed she was going to leave us. From that moment on, I played the role of the understander and made her feel that her actions were okay and necessary.

In the sixth grade, my school Westside Elementary was a small school, with a big play yard behind it. It was painted in a weird, green color. The majority of the grade-school was on the main floor except for the cafeteria, which was in the basement, but not much else – it must have had the world's most massive elementary school cafeteria. I did not feel committed to this school; the emotional connection I had with other classes before and after just wasn't there. The teachers were lackluster, and I cannot tell you any of their names.

My sisters attended Cheatham Park Elementary that year; it was a happy school with very short but wide green steps with flecks of sparkles leading to the classrooms. Artwork lined the hallways, and Deidre, the younger of the twins by five minutes, stayed there for two years. Both of them were in kindergarten, at least, for the first year. It was such a significant change for them as school is for many children who did not attend preschool or daycare. Spending most of the waking hours of the day with someone other than family is exciting to some children and problematic for others. My sisters adjusted to this change fairly well, especially considering the other changes at our house.

We attended the Cumberland Presbyterian church, Mt. Denson, on Highway 161 in the northeast part of Robertson County. The drive to the church was always the same – corn fields on each side of the long straight road bending upward as if to kiss the sky and lead you to heaven.

In its prime, Mt. Denson held about 150 people on Sunday mornings. The church pews were soft and matched the message of most of the sermons.

The lighting in the church was perfectly mute with the pink-stained glass windows letting through just enough light to bathe the average, country and city folk enjoying each other's fellowship. You would not find any saints in this church, just ordinary sinners who wanted a satisfying message on Sunday without too much toe stepping. There was always a friendly face and lots of hugging. A hug in the South is the equivalent of a handshake anywhere else in the country. The walls leading into the sanctuary were covered with pictures of the pastors who led the congregation. Many, many pastors' images lined the walls as the church had a way of not inviting a preacher to stay for more than a few years.

Springfield was a small community back in 1987, and the people hid all their warts. I can remember the stigma of being from a divorced home. I recall the feeling of shame when I went to friends' houses, of their moms hugging me closer than the rest of the kids, and the teachers being nicer to me because my parents were divorced. I remember seeing my dad cry because of my mom leaving – that was one of the very few times I had ever seen him cry. Later, I would see him cry at his mother's funeral and at my wedding. Tears did not come easy for that man, but when they did, they were significant.

That night in our kitchen, I was crying because Mom wasn't there with us. Dad sat down, held me close and told me it was ok to cry. I told him the same; he could cry, too. He said: **"I'll cry later tonight."** That was the first lesson I ever learned from him. While he was still human and had deep-felt emotions, he did not want to cry in front of his children who were also grieving. He understood that he needed to cry but not in the same space as us. There is a time for transparency and being vulnerable. However, there is also a time to be strong. My dad understood it was his time to be strong.

The first lesson Dad taught me was to *cry later*.

I also learned, however, that the opposite is true. When you do not pick the right time to cry, your value as a parent gets diluted. It's the same way for leaders. My father understood this concept even in 1987 before the modern-day leadership craze.

Unfortunately, I have found myself in situations where I did not discern the right time. For example, one Monday morning sitting in the conference room at the large mahogany table talking to my peers at work, I overshared the events of my weekend with them. I spoke openly about how tired I was (whining akin to crying), and immediately, I could feel my leadership quotient lessening.

My daughters and I had hiked almost twenty miles, and it was a great, physically demanding weekend. However, it left me unprepared to face the Monday that was standing before me. I sat down at the large wooden conference table where many decisions had been made before and where many would continue to be made. I sighed deeply and said, "I'm exhausted and should have taken today off; I'm just a wreck. My time management skills are not working today," and my saga continued to spill from my mouth. I did not apply wisdom in that situation.

Nevertheless, wisdom from others has shaped my life. The first lesson "*Cry Later*" shaped me. It helped me understand that there is a time to sob uncontrollably and a time to cry openly as I did the night Mom left. There is also a time to be the rock, the guide; this was the role Dad had to play on the first night after my mother left us, when I am sure he wanted to cry.

Dad did cry later. I can remember several weeks after that first night when I was sad about Mom leaving peeking in the kitchen and seeing him with our pastor from Mt. Denson. Dad was sitting at the same table where I cried with his back toward the door. The preacher was seated where he could see me. I stood a little distance from the doorway but close enough to see inside. I could see Dad's shoulders shaking – he was crying. I should not have been standing there. Dad had asked for privacy; he wanted to talk to our pastor alone. He needed to cry. This was his opportunity to cry later. The preacher and I made eye contact, but he did not let Dad know I was there. Dad had promised to cry later, and he did.

We all need someone with whom we can cry and grieve when necessary. We also need to know that in the age of transparency and sharing our emotions, we need to show discretion and find the right time to cry. For me, sitting in the conference room that day at work complaining at the wrong time was not the time to share how tired I was. I should have sucked it up and cried later.

> "To everything there is a season. A time for every purpose under heaven" Ecclesiastes 3:1 NKJV

There is a time for everything.
There is a time to cry.
There is a time to let others see you cry.
There is a time to be strong.

Leaders cry later. They choose the right time to cry.

L e s s o n 2

Always Take the Casserole

"For it is in giving that we receive." - *Francis of Assisi*

THE YEAR WAS 1987. Bobby Cox was the manager of the Atlanta Braves, leading them to the bottom of their division while playing in Atlanta's Fulton County Stadium. *Married with Children* and *The Simpsons* aired for the first time – changing the way the *American Dad* would be viewed forever. These shows portrayed the *American Dad* as a doofus without the ability to think for himself. It was dramatically different from the days of Andy Griffith, John Walton, and Charles Ingalls. The downfall of the *American Dad* had started in TV Land, but not in my small world. My dad was teaching me lessons every day.

The top-grossing movie of the year was *Three Men and a Baby* and Bon Jovi's *Living on a Prayer* was the #1 ranked song. It was also the year that I learned the second lesson from my father, ***always take the casserole.*** And in 1987, many dishes came to our house on Garner Street from our church.

"I'm so sorry about your wife leaving," she said. "Can you come to my car? I baked your family lunch; my special tuna casserole."

"Yes, ma'am," he said. "I'll be right there – girls, go get in the car, and I'll be back in a minute."

This charming church lady was the model for all other ladies at our church. She was a sweet, yet, sometimes meddling strong-willed lady in her 50s. She had her own family and grandchildren but took the time to make sure the work of the church was done to her liking. She wore bright red lipstick and a demure blue dress with sensible shoes and white gloves. After all, it was past Easter and not yet Labor Day, so it was perfectly fine to wear white in the South. Such rules, like when to wear white and when not to wear white mattered in the South.

Knowing her name was not necessary; she could have been any church lady. She was, in fact, every church lady. It was another Sunday and another church casserole. *How do they make sure we always have a meal on Sunday? Is someone keeping a list?*

"Always take the casserole," Dad said as he turned to me. He took yet another casserole from a little church lady from our church family. People want to help, and it never pays to tell someone you do not want their kindness. "Don't ever take that away from someone," he told us as he eased himself into the car and buckled his seatbelt. Some of those casseroles were quite good. Some, well, they were all appreciated. Dad just had to remember to return the dishes. He really liked it when they wrote their names on the top or bottom of the bowl on yellow masking tape.

It will never harm you to take the casserole. *Always take the casserole.*

We were the talk of Mt. Denson, a little country church Cumberland Presbyterian church. It was an experience residing in a small town in the Bible belt of the USA where little church ladies loved to talk about how terrible our situation was. Yet, loving us through this life-changing event by cooking us casseroles and giving us hugs and kisses that left traces of lipstick on our cheeks.

Always take the casserole was the second lesson from my father to me. The casserole can stand for many things in life. It can be a gift of someone buying dinner for you. It can be a kind word or advice that someone gives you.

Many times, Dad set the example and took the casserole. I'm sure it was hard for his ego to do so but it was a blessing for so many to help us. Think about how it feels to help someone and the benefits you receive.

People receive blessings when they do things for others. Making sure you allow them this grace is essential.

"Let love be without hypocrisy. Abhor what is evil. Cling to what is good. Be kindly affectionate to one another with brotherly love, in honor giving preference to one another; not lagging in diligence, fervent in spirit, serving the Lord; rejoicing in hope, patient in tribulation, continuing steadfastly in prayer; distributing to the needs of the saints, given to hospitality"(Romans 12:9-13 NKJV).

Now, as I think about this lesson that my dad taught me, I see its value in my life. Many times, I have not heeded this advice. I've not allowed someone the blessing of giving me a casserole, so to speak. I've been bullheaded and strong-willed. But pride cometh before the fall.

Pride plays a role in you not wanting to take the casserole, denying someone the opportunity to give you a blessing. You think to yourself, "I don't need your help." But people want to help and it does make them feel better about themselves when they do. It is a blessing to others when we allow them to help. Conversely, *when we help others, we feel better.*

A few weeks ago, my daughters put their Halloween costumes on and went to our neighbor's house. We live in what is called "the country" and our driveway is almost a half a mile long. So going to the neighbor's house isn't something you can do without thinking about it. The neighbors were waiting and ready for them. It was Halloween night and living where we do, we rarely have trick or treaters with our neighbors.

This particular year, Halloween was on a Tuesday, which meant it was on a school night. I left work early, raced to their school and then hurried home. We *only* had to get costumes changed, supper cooked and then walk up the driveway. This year, we had a peacock and a hippie. One day, my daughters will discover that other kids get to pick their costumes. Not my girls, we have an unveiling of the costumes.

Each year, I pick the costumes, not because I want to, but rather, it's just easier that way. This is one of my parenting tricks. I order the costumes and then we make it a big deal to have an "unveiling" – this is what you are going to be for Halloween.

I know many moms who have bought costumes early only for their precious children to decide they want to be something different. We never have that problem in my house.

As we walked out the door, my oldest child Amelia ran back into the house and grabbed something. Reagan followed her. I could not believe they were going back into the house. Sometimes, having children is like having kittens. Trying to get kids to do something fast is like getting the kittens to do something. It just isn't easy.

The girls showed me what they went back to the house to get. Amelia had a small prized possession to give to our neighbors – a rock. Reagan grabbed a pine cone she kept on her nightstand. They were, in fact, taking these gifts to our neighbors. These were the blessings they each wanted to give. It was their version of taking a southern casserole.

We walked out our back door and up the driveway. Amelia led the way with her small rock in her hand. Reagan stayed back with me and held my hand as we walked up the path. Amelia, nine, and Reagan, seven; they are sisters who are great friends, yet, very, very different. Amelia is a great adventurer. Reagan would prefer to adventure with me.

After our quick walk up the driveway, we arrived at our neighbor's house. They had gifts for each of the girls. Thoughtfully purchased admissions to our local zoo. My daughters proudly gave the gifts to our neighbors. The pride on the girls' faces was so visible that you could tell from the expression on my neighbors' face they knew these were prized possessions they were being given.

Always take the casserole.

I am so thankful that our neighbors took the small tokens from the girls.

At times in our lives, God sends people with the casseroles.

"And My God shall supply all your need according to His riches in glory by Christ Jesus" – Philippians 4:19 NKJV

In Philippians 4:19, we are reminded that God will supply our needs. Not necessarily our wants. But He, the great provider will provide. He will bring people into our lives to nourish us both in spirit and in comfort.

On the other hand, there are times when we need to be the person who takes the casserole. It's our responsibility to pay it forward when we can. And more importantly, we should do for others even when we don't feel like it. The best way to beat the blues is to do something for others. It will lift your mood, brighten your day and help someone out.

Part II:
Wisdom from an Adventurous Parent

Lesson 3

Sleep Later

"As soon as I saw you, I knew adventure was going to happen." - Winnie the Pooh

WE SPENT MANY TUESDAYS AND Saturday afternoons at Opryland with my dad during the summer of 1989 and 1990, after our annual season passes were purchased. Opryland was an amusement park in Nashville from 1972 to 1997. Sadly, after 1997, it was dismantled and replaced by a mall. These annual passes to Opryland were a rite of passage for locals; you were not a real local if you did not have a season pass.

The early passes were just a plastic card, similar to a credit card, without the raised numbers. Initially, the cards did not have a picture to identify the cardholder, but Opryland got wise, and in the later years, they required a photo on their season passes. The truth is there may have been some "sharing" of passes to help out those who weren't fortunate to have a pass; thus, the picture requirement. But there was not any sharing for us; our passes were purchased fair and square. My dad would never have jeopardized his or our good name for a free day at Opryland.

At the beginning of summer, Dad took my sisters and me to Wal-Mart where he lovingly bought all our clothes except for church dresses. Our church dresses were always purchased from Castner Knott or JC Penny at Rivergate Mall. Church dress shopping was a serious event and always done around Christmas and Easter to coincide with holidays and band recitals. Each of us played in the school concert band, and the dress code for these concerts was "church attire."

These trips were made especially to buy our dresses. I'm sure Dad felt out of place in the department stores, but he never showed it. Dad always had an excellent eye for dresses, and he was proud that he could buy them. He knew how to pick dresses that would last, look pretty and flatter each of our different personalities. This was our one splurge and they were most beautiful. They were a cut above the regular dresses being both expensive and pretty. We never had a lot of lovely dresses, but the ones he bought were purchased with care by him.

There was a special trip each year to buy our Opryland outfits. Each year, he bought each of us a pair of shoes and an outfit just for Opryland. A smart man he was in many things, but he was exceptionally wise when it came to setting up our environment for fun. He knew that by the end of summer these shoes and clothes would be ruined, and he did not want us damaging our "good" clothes at the park.

Dad was off on Tuesdays and always took us to Opryland. We also spent almost every Saturday there after he got off work at noon in Springfield. We had a 45-minute drive filled with anticipation of spending the day at the magical park. Those days were full, on purpose. Dad knew that if we were busy and tired by the end of the day, we would sleep well.

Many nights, my sisters fell asleep in the back of our beige Jeep Cherokee after a full day in the heat at the amusement park while Dad and I listened to the Oldies station play songs by The Beach Boys and Elvis. Dad worked hard to make our memories as magical as he could on a limited salary and time with us. "Dad, why do we go so hard on the weekend?" I asked him. He responded, "Because you can *sleep later.*" That's the next lesson I learned from my dad. Sleep was something you could do later.

I remember Dad planning our yearly summer camping trip. But I broke my arm. I had just spent a week at Crystal Springs Church Camp in Kelso, TN with my church friends from other Cumberland Presbyterian Churches in Tennessee. I had a wonderful week with other Christians without any incidents – until I was almost home.

As I waited to be picked up from camp, I decided it would be fun to climb a tree with my friends from my local church. We found a tree on the Brentwood Cumberland Presbyterian grounds that was longing to be climbed. Before I knew it, my foot slipped on a crooked tree limb and I fell hitting the ground with a solid "thud." Immediately, the pain ran through my body like a lightning strike.

I knew something was wrong. Really wrong. My left arm was aching in a way that I had never experienced before. My week at the church camp was magical – spending time in the natural environment with fellow young adults was a faith strengthener for me. And this was not the best way to end that wonderful week.

"Damnit," my father said when he found out I'd broken my arm. Damnit was the only cuss word he ever said. But when he said it, he meant it, and we knew he was mad.

"Dad, are you taking me camping with you?" I asked with a bit of trepidation in my voice.

"No, sorry. Can't take you with me if you have a broken arm." And that is what caused him to say, "damnit." I was messing up the fun for the week.

That summer, during the family vacation, I stayed with my mom while Dad took my sisters and cousin camping. I do remember the awful feeling of being left out but if you could not play hard, you could not be a part of the fun. *Sleep later* could only be accomplished when you are healthy and ready for an adventure.

Camping was fun. Dad made it enjoyable. Even when it rained, it was fun. Our days spent camping were filled with hikes and memory making. But it would not have been fun to take along a kid who wasn't at 100%. Breaking my arm taught me for the first time what a terrible nurse my dad was – if you wanted sympathy, you needed to look somewhere else. This may seem like a paradox because Dad is such a caring man, and it is. But Dad loved to have fun and that required you to be 100%.

Two summers before I broke my arm and missed that week of camping, my dad let me in on a secret.

"Come here," he said to me after my sisters went to bed, his tone full of wonder. My sisters were eight at the time and I was thirteen. For two years, our summer vacations had consisted of those season passes to Opryland. We had finally settled into a family of four and had our own routine of fun, even without my mom.

"Look at this." He said, giddy as a kid at Christmas. "What is it?" I asked him. I was in my pajamas with my hair in a ponytail. Dad and I always watched one TV show after my sisters went to bed. It was precious time that he could spend with just me. One on one time was limited in our household, and he worked hard to make every one of those moments count with each of us. We all had cherished one on one time with Dad. He worked hard to speak to us in our own love language.

"It's a tent," he finally said, using the most of the moment to build the excitement; his face lit up like I had never seen before. Dad was a funny practical joker, but he did not exhibit personal joy often. He was usually happy with what we did and was proud of us but he rarely had moments where he was proud of himself. His life was so focused on providing and making a living for his three girls.

"This year, instead of getting season passes to Opryland, I'm going to buy camping equipment and then next year, we will go camping. Will that be ok?" he asked. I could tell he wanted me to be as excited as he was about camping. I was eager but also a little disappointed about Opryland. But I would never let him know I was a bit sad. Disappointing my dad was not something I ever wanted to do at that age; I understood that as much then as I do now.

For many years after he bought that first tent, we camped in the Great Smoky Mountains National Park. We spent a week tent camping and adventurously used a "white gas" stove. A white gas stove is a camping stove that requires a special fuel in a rectangular aluminum can and purchased from an outdoor store. Dad was always nervous traveling with the fuel and never took it home with us, worried it would blow up in the car on the way home, but oddly we typically brough it with us, guess he wasn't afraid it would blow up on the way there!

I have so many beautiful memories of the days we spent camping – memories of spitting off bridges, hiking, cooking one-pot meals for supper meaning canned beef stew, chicken and dumplings, and anything else that could be dumped from a can over bread or crackers. These meals could not have tasted any better and felt like they were gourmet. We never had these meals at home, except once. Dad purchased Sue Bee chicken and dumplings for us to have at home, and it was terrible. It was magical at camp because we were hungry. All the food tasted so good after a hard day of play in the Great Smoky Mountains National Park in East Tennessee and Western North Carolina.

family and rested a bit knowing we needed to be set up for success for Sunday's day of fun. Sunday we have plans to hike to the top of Roan Mountain – on the balds. The balds are areas that my dad loved to frequent; I could not appreciate why until I got a little older.

As a child, hiking to the top of a mountain that had no trees at its summit seemed weird. Why would you hike up to someplace that has no trees? I could not quite comprehend that the beauty was the absence of the trees and the incredible view it afforded you.

The mountain allows you to see this view when it chooses. The best days are when it is crystal clear; those days in East Tennessee are few. Most are hazy on the mountain. But today our view is perfect. Today, we choose to play hard and *sleep later*, soaking up every moment of this beautiful day.

That trip with my daughters was magical in a way because I was able to take them with my sister Danielle to a particular place where Dad took my sisters and me camping and hiking, Roan

Mountain. Danielle and I have taken my daughters on such grand adventures that when we came back all we could do was rest; these are the best types of experiences. *Sleep later.* We have heeded Dad's wisdom to sleep later. We know that there is always time in life to do chores, fold laundry, and wash dishes. And these chores must be done but adventure must also be had. Adventure awaits.

I want my daughters to remember the adventurous times just as I remember the times camping with my dad. Often, we would load the car on Friday nights when Dad got off work, then wake up early the next morning and head out, camping all weekend, making memories, and taking pictures. A reminder that life isn't just the daily grind, but it's the adventures that make it great.

Lesson 4

Just Keep Walking

"Keep your face always toward the sunshine – and the shadows will fall behind you." - Walt Whitman

"HELLO, DONITA, THIS IS YOUR DAD."

Did he say those words?

He identified himself as my father, the man whose voice I know anywhere? It was a voicemail I would replay many times in my mind even years later. He said "hello." That is such a weird way to leave a voicemail. No one is going to reply when you say, "hello" on a voicemail. But my dad had, has and always will have impeccable manners; a root of his upbringing.

He always said that it did not cost anything to be nice. He felt the need to offer a greeting on the voicemail the way he thought it necessary to say "hello" and look people in the eye when he spoke to them. Each morning, when I lived under his roof, he always said, "good morning," never allowing the familiarity of the family setting to remove the common courtesy of being polite.

Many mornings, this polite, southern gentleman with a wiry mustache would say, "good morning" to my sisters and me only to be greeted with a grunt and barely an acknowledgment of his presence when we were teenagers. He kept one of my sisters' troll dolls in the kitchen. The troll doll with its fuzzy hair shaped in a pink cone to a tip and goofy looking smile sitting on the paper towel holder above our sink.

I noticed it, most likely after it had been there for weeks, and inquired why he put it there. He told me quietly that when he looked at it, it made him smile. My dad always had a reason for everything he did and this was no different. The troll doll was there to make him smile. He used small, everyday things to brighten his days and those of others. He could look at this doll and its goofy expression would make him smile when life didn't. Honestly, my sisters and I were not always easy to parent or to love. Raising three girls under one roof, especially during our teenage years was not always comfortable. Parenting is hard work, and parenting teenagers is not for the faint of heart.

The days are long in parenting but the years are short.

"Donita." He said my name on the voicemail. I wondered if he did this just in case the wrong person, someone other than me picked up the message. I have always loved how he said my odd name. With love. Correct pronunciation. Emphasis on the "DON-e-ta."

Unlike my father, my manners are not polished and often, in my hurry to complete a task, I may seem a bit brash. I remember thinking that he wasted 5 seconds by saying, "Hello, Donita..."

Now, as I am older and a little bit wiser, I realize his manners and the extra seconds it took him to be nice were not wasted. Rather, this was a gift he could give others, much like the gift of a smile he gave himself each morning when he saw the troll doll in the kitchen with its goofy grin.

Did he think I wouldn't know it was him? I have heard him say "Donita," many times through the years. Of course, at that point, he was my father for more than 30 years. My rock when life got crazy; he was always there, steady. He called my name while comforting, counseling, and reprimanding me. How could I not know?

"Donita," he said sternly one day he met me on the front porch of our house after we had both returned home. "If I ever see you drive like that again, I will call your insurance company." I knew

I had screwed up. "Donita, I cannot take your car away; you bought it," he said angrily. His voice was firm; he did not yell but it wasn't gentle either. "But you were a danger to yourself and others." He was right.

I saw him on the road and thought it would be funny to pass him on the small back road we lived on in my 1968 Brittany Blue mustang that ran, most of the time. I was seventeen years old and coming home from working a shift at Ponderosa Steakhouse as a waitress. He had picked my sisters up from band practice. Dad did not laugh or think it was funny to put us all in danger.

"This is your Dad." At that time, phones were not "smart" they were "dumb" and were only used to place calls and send texts. My quiet, shy, loving, small in stature father is very wise. As I was growing up in my small town, he frequently told me when he sent me on errands in the city, "Tell them who you are." In other words, tell them you are my daughter. They will treat you better than if they do not know who you are. He was right. His family identification and honor-worthy name meant something. No one in our town ever had a harsh word to say about my dad.

He has had many names throughout the years. Ken Taylor, Optician at Springfield Optical for almost forty years. The man who would stay late to fix glasses, make house calls to shut-ins, drive to nursing homes or the local hospital.

My sisters and I went on many house calls with him. Often, after he had worked a full day, picked us up from the babysitter's house and still had an entire night's worth of chores. There was always homework, supper to prepare and little girls to get to bed before cleaning up and getting ready for the next day.

Dad was also an elder at Mt. Denson Cumberland Presbyterian Church. A role that caused him many sleepless nights due to the decisions that had to be made on behalf of the church. He has often said to me, if you want to make someone mad, do it at church; that's where everything can get blown out of proportion. He helped the church decide on new preachers, building campaigns, what to do about the youth group, and other ordinary church administrative decisions.

However, he took these decisions seriously and never made one without a lot of thought.

He was a member of the Springfield Lions Club where giving back mattered, even when he had little money and little time as the single-divorced father of three girls. It was tough but when there was always something to do, he made time to do what mattered. He volunteered when he did not have the time. Do you know what that meant? His three rambunctious girls had to go along with him.

I can so fondly remember the practices for the Springfield Lions Club Minstrel Shows when the dress rehearsals went for three nights before the actual show. These were highly regarded practice sessions, and it was considered an honor to attend. He would sit us in the front row with our homework while he participated in the dress rehearsal.

He had been Kim's, (my mom) first husband and one of many men she married. Even though Mom was married several times, she loved us, and we loved her. These marriages, until they took her away from us physically, did not seem odd to us.

We did not know they should have been; we figured this was just the life we lived.

After the first divorce, we were already different from most of our friends at school and definitely different from our friends at church. The husbands and boyfriends that came and went were always good to us. My dad was the gracious ex-husband, offering to share holidays, Thanksgiving and Christmas, where we had what we termed "dysfunctional family holidays." Mom, her husband at the time, my dad, and the three girls shared a meal, opened presents, and spent time together.

Dad had four siblings; he was the youngest of the group. Eighteen years between the oldest to the youngest solidified my dad's place among the group as the prankster. When they were all together, shenanigans were always expected. And guess who was the instigator most of the time? My dad.

He was the youngest son of Edith and Horty Taylor, from Elizabethton, TN, a town he loved that was close to the mountains. It called at his soul but he chose to leave when I was born so he could make more money to support his growing family.

Dad is also the friend to many, a keen listener when needed. His quiet nature, great listening skills and the wise advice he was known to give encouraged many people to stop by his office. He always seemed to take the time to listen to others, especially his children.

He never told me he did not have the time to listen when I needed an ear. During my college years, I broke up with a boyfriend. "The one," I thought, but thankfully he was not. My dad sat with me on the front porch, held my hand and let me cry on his shoulder; my big tears wet his shirt. He held my hand for what seemed like hours, did not require me to talk, and he did not find the need to speak; he just sat there with me.

His office on Willow Street in Springfield boasted a comfortable, old, green, worn out recliner he kept in the back corner of his office. If it could talk, it would recount many problems, relive many tears shed and relate much of the wise advice Dad gave. My daughters love to curl up in this chair and talk to their Pappy.

The cell phone was a technology he could not quite understand at the time. Why people felt the need to have cell phones and talk on them as they were driving eluded him until many years later when he found himself on a long commute using this technology to speak with his daughters, at least, once a day while he drove. Sometimes, on this commute, he would tell me, "I need to put the phone down for a minute, hold on," while he merged into or got out of traffic.

It was annoying at first as I wondered why my dad could not just talk and drive. Nevertheless, I realized he wanted to focus on what he was doing; one thing at a time. It kept him safe in his car. Dad has never been a multi-tasker, plus, driving and talking on the phone was something that made little sense to him. Regardless of the technology accessories he was given such as a Bluetooth state of the art headset, he liked to hold the phone in his hand while he talked on it as if he was holding the person with whom he conversed.

He has never been an early adopter of technology. Ironically, this enduring quality, the anti-technology stance, came from a man who later would have a daughter (me) working in the field of information technology. Often, Dad would tell me not to try explaining the work I did. He claimed he could not understand it; however, I knew that he could and most likely did, but in some odd way, I believe he pretended not to, in order to make me feel smart and worthy of the many years I spent in school.

He was also the father of his three girls and a grandfather of two. I knew it was my dad on the voicemail that day and I was grateful that God chose him to be my father.

That day while hiking when he introduced himself on the phone, "Donita, this is your father," he was presenting the role he was playing that day. I will never understand why he felt the need to tell me who he was during this call. And even though I asked him once, I never received an answer. He just smiled with tight lips and shrugged his broad shoulders.

I was listening to my messages on my cell phone, thinking that I must have been, at least, halfway up to the top of Mt. LeConte, traveling up Trillium Gap Trail. He had dropped me off at the trailhead and he and his best friend, Bill, had traveled to the trailhead on the other side of the mountain. They were hiking up Alum Cave Trail.

Alum Cave is my dad's favorite trail to the top. Mt. LeConte was and has been an extraordinary place to our family. Each year, we hike to the summit of the mountain celebrating our birthdays there. And this year was no different, we were hiking up to the top and as usual, with five trails to the top, we did not hike together. Each of us in our hiking crew moves at a different pace. We respect the need for other hikers to do their own hike, meaning to hike at their own pace. We would meet at the top, spend the night and then journey down together.

I dug my phone out of my backpack; a trusted friend it is though borrowed from Dad. He is the resident backpack loaner. Anyone who needs a pack can find one to borrow from Him. Like rain jackets (he owned many), he purchased backpacks frequently from REI – always from there – never anywhere else. He remained their loyal supporter even when the drive to their store was a hardship, being more than an hour away from our small town.

He loved REI and said "it had good air" that the people were nice, happy, and genuine. When he visited their store, he would pause at the front door, take a deep breath and say, "They just have good air in here," then he would walk around the store in the same logical fashion each time, always going in the same direction.

Dad never found the "one." He always thought the next backpack would be better than the previous one. The backpack I was sporting was black with two zipper pockets, one large and one small. The small zipper pocket held my cell phone in a trusted Ziploc sandwich bag in case it rained. I struggled to get the phone out of the Ziploc sandwich bag, which was in a Ziploc gallon bag. Hiking in the Smokies is like summer in Florida; you never know when there will be a pop-up shower. And we believed in placing essential items, like cell phones in a Ziploc sandwich bag, in another Ziploc gallon bag and then in a backpack. This multiple bag approach has saved our electronics many times while hiking and getting caught in a rainstorm.

"Donita, I dropped you off at the wrong trailhead; you've got to walk about 2.5 miles to get to the one that I should have left you at, but you have all your water and food, so you should be ok."

What was he saying?

Was he serious?

This is a hard hike!

I should have been halfway up the trail based on my time; instead, I was about 1/3 of the way up. Not a huge setback but I had to pick up my pace to make it to the top to meet my dad and his friend Bill.

My dad's birthday is on July 19th; my sisters' on July 12th and mine on July 16th. Our annual hike is where we share many birthday cakes, cards, and wishes. As we all got older, we understood that time spent together away from the distractions of the world was the best gift we could give one another. There are so many fond memories of us sitting on the front porch of our cabin at the top of Mt. LeConte after our hikes, talking about the miles we had covered and catching up on life in general.

Sometimes, our annual trips to the top were filled with friends who hiked with us; other times, it was just family. Each trip was different but meaningful and part of our family DNA. Our annual trek to the top of the mountain is our yearly marathon. We trained for it all year; we talked about what gear we were going to take and which trail we were going to travel to the top. The planning of the hike was as enjoyable as the hike itself.

The Lodge accommodates 60+ people in the cabins. Some of the cabins hold as few as four people while some hold more than ten. Inside the cabins are all the same, double bunk beds. As you walk into the cabins, you pass the front porch that each boasts. These front porches greet their tired hikers with a welcoming rise and rocking chairs that feel so good after a long hike. Many stories about the trails are shared on these front porches.

Inside the wooden cabins, warmed with propane heat and lit with oil lamps are dark from the lack of electricity – but that is part of its rustic charm. The beds have wool blankets on them and the white sheets are carried up and down the mountain by a team of llamas every other day. It's a sight to behold; a trail of llamas carrying the hikers' supplies. The beds squeak, especially when you climb on to the top bunk by scaling a short wooden ladder affixed by screws to the cot.

Rivaled by Clingman's Dome, which sits at 6643 feet above sea level, the elevation at Mt. LeConte is 6,593 feet. It is the second highest elevation in the Great Smoky Mountains National Park.

The people at the top of the mountain are different from those you see in the towns at the base of the mountain. Gatlinburg, Pigeon Forge, and Sevierville hold shoppers and families who look forward to playing mini-golf. While these are great people, there is a bit of normalcy seen in those mountain towns that attracts those who want to be close to the mountains but not in the mountains.

Mountain people are different from vacationers. Mountain people feel the need to answer the call of the mountain as if the air from it can breathe life into you that you cannot get from anywhere else. Its serenity is amazing, especially while speaking to your soul on the mountain trail as if the mountain says, "It's all going to be ok; I am here with you." The same way Dad's gentle spirit comforts many, the mountain is the spirit animal of my dad.

The trees turn their leaves up to catch the sun and the rain. The rocks keep the soul grounded on the trail and the air on the dear and precious mountain fills the lungs with a life-giving breath, which cannot be inhaled anywhere except in the mountain. The call of the mountain tugs at one's soul. "And when He had sent them away, He departed to the mountain to pray" (Mark 6:46 NKJV). Christ went to the mountains to pray after He and the disciples fed the 5,000 using the five loaves and two fishes. He modeled that rest and rejuvenation vital to recharge one's soul.

Many who hike find themselves on Mt. LeConte and staying at the Lodge on the top of the mountain. They either call it a one-time adventure and never return or immediately plan their next hike up the mountain.

You can tell those who love the peace of the mountain and the hike to Mt. LeConte by their determination to make each step count and soak up every moment on the trail from the first step they take on the journey. The path becomes a part of their souls.

The people who work on the top of the mountains stay there for several days at a time and live in cabins similar to those the hikers stay in. The staff has a different spirit about them; they are mountain people. The people who traverse to the top of the mountain are kindred spirits, sharing tables with one another in a family style dinner and breakfast setting. The Lodge serves dinner the night you hike up and breakfast the next morning. Dinner conversations frequently center on what happened on the hike up to the Lodge and how many times each person has climbed the mountain.

The food served by the Lodge staff always tastes like a 7-course gourmet meal. In the more than fifteen years that my family has been hiking to the top of Mt. LeConte, the dinner and breakfast menus have not changed. For dinner, it is always broccoli cheese soup, roast beef with gravy, mashed potatoes, cornbread, green beans with little onions and cinnamon apples. Breakfast is scrambled eggs with Canadian bacon sliced on top, biscuits, pancakes, and grits.

The meals are so delicious, they could only have been prepared by angels. They taste so good partly because you are hungry from the hike and anything would taste good and because the adventure of getting to the top makes everything a little bit more magical. The food is served family style while we sit at large tables and meet new people. Interacting with others who have just shared the same experience and kept walking makes the meal abundantly joyful.

The dining room is lit with oil lamps, as no electricity is available on top of the mountain. The lighting makes the room glow warmth as the sun sets. The dining room itself is paneled with dark wood and the tables are long with straight back wooden chairs that any other time would feel hard but after a tough hike, they are welcoming.

The cabins each facing the dining hall welcome each hiker as they intermingle with each other saying their hellos and resting their weary feet.

The first year my dad got a reservation, I was not able to go with him; as his hiking partner, I was devastated. My professor in my MBA program would not allow me to take an exam early. I had to do so at the same time as everyone else. My sister, Danielle, not in her hiking prime went with my dad. On later trips, she almost sprinted to the top, fueled by her love for the trail after weight loss surgery; she took my spot on this hike.

That first year was a challenging one for both my dad and Danielle to hike. It is a hard hike until you decide to stop battling the trail and work with it. It is harder than necessary until you choose to embrace the journey. Hiking is not as physical as it is a mental game. You must decide you are not going to conquer the mountain but become part of it, allowing its path to meld with your own.

That first year was a landmark year; Dad has not missed a year of hiking that trail since 2004.

We had planned to walk Trillium Gap with Naomi and her son Erik who were more like members of our family than just friends.

"Donita, *just keep walking.* I'll see you at the top." I shut off my phone as I sat on the trail with Naomi and Erik and gave them the news. "Dad and Bill dropped us off at the wrong trailhead," I said.

They looked at me with their eyes wide open; they knew we had a few more miles ahead of us than planned. Naomi is a diabetic and had managed the disease for more than 40 years at that point. We had only intended to be on the trail for a certain amount of miles; it was a setback. Naomi's knees were also not in the best condition and each additional step on the steep path after about 5 or 6 miles would be painful. We had at least 8 to 10 miles total to hike.

My dad was already on his trail, Alum Cave Trail. It was shorter but also steep. At 5.5 miles, Alum Cave Trail has an elevation gain of 2,763 feet. Majestic views line the path and it's the most famous of the 5 trails to the top of Mt. LeConte. This trail bodes areas such as "Alum Cave Bluff," a dusty cave that many people hike on. While that is rustically beautiful, the remaining portion of the hike for 2.8 miles is even more magnificent than just the bluff itself.

He dropped me off at Rainbow Falls, which is close to the trail we had planned to hike. Close, but not quite there. We planned; therefore, we were going to execute that plan because that's what Taylors do – they plan and stick to the plan – they *just keep walking.*

The hike should have been around 7 miles, with 3,401 feet of elevation gain. We added an additional 2.5 miles before we actually got to the trailhead.

Naomi and her family became our friends when my sisters were in middle school in the 1990s. Naomi and her husband Bill have a set of twins who are the same age as my sisters; parents of twins gravitate towards each other, and as a bonus, this family started attending our church, Mt. Denson Cumberland Presbyterian Church. They were also hikers, and our families shared many hikes and vacations together through the years.

Naomi was my math tutor in high school. Math was not a subject I ever really enjoyed, but she made it fun. She had the ability to show me how to take complex problems and turn them into something easy to understand. She made time for me and whatever needed to be discussed, whether it was school, work, math problems and later in life, children. Over the years, she has transitioned from a mother figure to me to a friend I cherish dearly.

Friendships that develop with people who were initially your teachers or mentors are gifts in life; they are rare. The majority of people who come into your life are like the leaves on a tree during a hike. They are there for a period of time and serve a purpose; they are not there for a long time to withstand the test of time. Friends whose relationships have transitioned and developed over a period of time-share parts of each other, like the hiking trail itself.

Over the years, I have been blessed with many people who have stayed for a season but were not there for long; we all learned something from the interaction. But people who are in your life for the long haul are like the mountain itself.

As I shared this hike with Naomi, I learned this next valuable lesson from my father, *"just keep walking.*" I reflect on this hike and other times in life and recall how Naomi helped me to keep walking both literally on this hike in the Great Smoky Mountains National Park and theoretically in life decisions when college algebra and calculus seemed to elude me.

Just keep walking. Those words have stuck with me several times in life. Just keep walking. Life is not always comfortable. Life is still worth it. The best plans are like the hike I went on; it was hard and took extra effort. Effort I never intended to spend. But it was worth it. Looking back, I realize it is the hardest parts of the hike I remember most. Just like in life, the challenges make the experiences most interesting. Those words from my dad, "*just keep walking*" sit at the front of my thoughts whenever I feel like giving up.

Just keep walking. One foot in front of the other. Forward motion, forward progress. Each step is a step closer to the top of the mountain, whatever the mountain you are climbing may be.

Like that first week home from the hospital with Amelia, my oldest, I needed my dad's advice.

"Dad, this is hard," I said with my first child in my arms. I was at home with Amelia. She cried. All. The. Time. Cried in the morning. Cried at night. Cried at noon. The only time she did not cry was when I was holding her, and she was nursing. It was a harrowing experience for me. She was 3 days old. I sobbed uncontrollably. And trust me, it was not pretty; I do not cry pretty. My face was splotchy. I was a mess, and frankly, we were all a mess.

My husband had hand surgery two weeks before I gave birth; although he is a "doer" and does not let anything get in the way of accomplishing work, however, life with a newborn was hard for a family with four hands, let alone our family with three.

Amelia was the child I did not think I would be able to have. After two miscarriages, I was fearful of losing her and worried about being a first-time mom. Robert and I were married for eight years before we were blessed with this viable pregnancy. Married in our 20s, we did not feel the pull to be parents until close to our 30s. We lost two precious babies whom we would never hold on this earth. *Just keep walking*. The third time was the charm.

Our pregnancy losses occurred early – one at eight weeks and another at fourteen. Despite that, we were left with a hole in our hearts. We wondered if we would ever have children. I knew that was all that would satisfy me – a child to hold in my arms, to count his or her fingers and toes, to take on the hiking trail and teach the lessons of life.

Would I be a good mother? Would I be enough for her? I prayed every day for this child. I was on bed rest at 30 weeks and gave birth at 37 weeks. Amelia was the child I did not think would ever come into my life. Now, I realize that much like the hike to the top of the summit of Mt. LeConte, the journey, putting one foot in front of the other to just keep walking, is the most critical lesson of parenting.

"Donita, it is going to be ok. You will be ok," he told me. *Just keep walking.*

The first year with Amelia was hard. Harder than anything I had ever done. It was harder than getting my college degree in accounting from

Austin Peay University in Clarksville, TN. Harder than landing my first job. Harder than earning my Masters of Business Administration. Harder than each of these because the demands of parenting were unknown to me. I had never spent any real time with a baby. I had two sisters who were five years younger than me, and I knew how to help with them but I was not the type of person who enjoyed being around kids.

I would be envious of those who came up with games at the spur of the moment to play with a group of kids at church or at parties. Jealous of those who were highly coveted to babysit. But that was not me. Until I had my own child, I could not remember a time that I had held a baby for longer than what was considered to be appropriate so I wouldn't appear to be rude when someone said, "Would you like to hold him/her?"

Yet, parenting has been more rewarding than any of those accomplishments. *Just keep walking.*

Lesson 5

Good Day or a GREAT Day

"Your living is determined not so much by what life brings to you as by the attitude you bring to life; not so much by what happens to you as by the way your mind looks at what happens"-
Khalil Gibran

"GOOD MORNING!" MY DAD SAID jovially as he dressed for his morning walk. That was nothing extraordinary. He was always proud of the fact that walking did not take any special equipment. He was wearing Nikes, khakis and a t-shirt – his morning uniform. He had already been up for about two hours.

Drinking his coffee before the house started stirring and reading his Bible. He had a set morning routine. Always the same. Review the to-do list, drink coffee, read the Bible, and pray. Somewhere in there, he read his bucket list. He'd written down a list of items he wanted to do, which today would be termed a "bucket list" but thirty years ago it wasn't called that. He was ahead of his time.

On the list, he had written many things; he was a practical dreamer. The only item I remember was "ride in a hot air balloon," and that's the one I have always wanted to surprise him with. I guess you could consider that an item on my bucket list, too! My sisters and I found this list several years ago while we were rummaging through his stuff when he was selling his house, reminding me of all the times I had looked at this list growing up. Each time I looked at his bucket list, I felt as if I were reading something I shouldn't, which, of course, was true. I shouldn't have been reading it.

His list intrigued me, and I have always wondered what prompted him to write it. Now, I understand the importance of lists.

There's something magical about writing down your desires. By putting your goals on paper, there's a good chance of having one of two things happen. 1) You will accomplish them. 2) You will decide they aren't worth achieving and take them off the list.

"*Grrr,*" I said, back when Dad greeted me. I was never a morning person; instead, I was often a porcupine, bristling when my dad tried to hug me in the morning. I was standing in our kitchen in my pajamas, barefoot with my eyes sleepy and my hair a mess. He was leaving to go on his morning walk. My sisters were then in grade school, and I was in middle school.

My dad walked every morning. He was a modified fair-weather walker. He did not walk in the rain but hot or cold did not bother him. His daily morning walks were his solace then and still are now. He uses them to clear his thoughts and think about the day. It is the one part of his day when he does not have to think about the issues, what needed to be done or to do things for others. These walks allowed him to put one foot in front of the other, letting the pavement serve as his therapy.

I wish I had taken the opportunity when he asked me many times to walk with him but I always felt like I was too busy. "Too busy" should be an offensive phrase. I know I have missed out on many meaningful events in life because I was "too busy." Looking back, I wonder what was so important that I felt I was too busy to do the significant things. Why was I too busy to spend time with those who mattered the most to me?

These days, with a family of my own, I often let "too busy" interfere with the precious moments I have to spend with my family. I am saddened by my own lost opportunities to play Candyland, go on bike rides, watch TV, or just snuggle with my daughters. Does the feeling of satisfaction that comes from answering yet one more email from work, writing one more paper, doing one more chore make life better? In reality, it rarely does. As I reflect on the many times I missed walking with my dad, when I was "too busy," I cannot fathom what was more important. Hindsight is always 20/20.

I guess I was too busy talking to one of my friends on the phone at that point in my life. We only had a land line with a cord that was stretched to almost smooth from its original curly state. I could have been busy reading a novel. Or, possibly sleeping. None of these activities should have replaced quality time with my father. But who actually appreciates their parents when they're young? Only the wise.

"My son, hear the instruction of your father, And do not forsake the law of your mother; For they will be a graceful ornament on your head, And chains about your neck" (Proverbs 1:8-9 NKJV).

My dad left my sisters and me to get ready each morning. He learned that the best offense of a father-led house is a good defense – fewer arguments that way. He learned early as a single parent of school-age children, especially girls, that if he were there in a house that had one bathroom while we got ready for school, limbs would be lost.

Many mornings, everything was just terrible. It seemed more natural to let us fight it out on our own. I was never a morning person and was especially mean to my sisters, for spite. I was the oldest and clung tightly to the power of that position.

One morning, I was trying to get into the bathroom first to be especially mean. I intended to strut my oldest sister status. I stayed in the bathroom so long, on purpose, it caused my sister to pee on herself. I could have let her into the bathroom to use it. Now, it's beyond me why I was so mean. I made her wait painfully for me to get out of the shower.

As I transport myself to this moment, I can see the look of anguish on her face and how I felt like the worst person in the world. However, my actions spoke differently. I covered my feelings up with a terse word about how she needed to get up earlier to get to the bathroom before me. The look on her face will never leave my memory and reminds me that I traded this moment, which I can't ever get back, for one of misery.

But during these trying times, my sisters and I learned that we had to solve our own arguments. Dad was out walking while we were getting ready. He was such a smart man.

He got in his walk and left the house during the most terrible time of the day when three females were in the house. Our house technically had two bathrooms but the upstairs bathroom never worked well. It was so typically out of commission and inoperative, we finally decided not to use it. Probably someone who was handier than my dad might have been able to fix it but it was one of those items that got lower priority than the other needs our big rambling house had at the time.

Mornings were tough. If you have ever doubted there is a devil, journey to a house with children during the morning hours when everyone is trying to get to their respective places and watch.

Throughout the school year, my sisters and I stayed with our dad. Three girls. Weekdays. It was up to him to do homework, get lunch money together, work on school projects, and run the school taxi.

Dad decided to make the school taxi a place where we could set the intentions for a good day. He planted many seeds in the car ride to school. The seeds he planted helped us realize that it was up to us to have a good day or a great day.

"But these are the ones sown on good ground, those who hear the word, accept it, and bear fruit: some thirtyfold, some sixty, and some a hundred" (Mark 4:20 NKJV).

We loaded up in the car to make the morning school taxi run. My sisters were at one school (although there were years where they were each in separate schools, leaving my dad to pick up and drop off at three different schools in our town), and I was at another. He learned to efficiently and effectively utilize our time in the car, as he optimized our routes making sure he spent the least amount of time possible in the vehicle. As a working parent, he could not spend all morning in the car. He still had to put in a full day's work after he dropped us off. I am sure that sometimes, he thought work was a small escape for him after our terrible, no good mornings.

Being a family of one parent and three kids, the front seat was a hot commodity. Everyone wanted to sit in the front seat of Dad's beige Jeep Cherokee. The front seat was the seat of power because it was the seat closest to Dad. In the front seat, you could have conversations with Dad that seemed to be impossible from the back seat.

Sitting in the front, you were the chief navigator, the helper, the go-to person for all things for Dad. Dad was very methodical and fair in how he approached most decisions in life and who got to sit in the front seat of the car was dealt with in a similar fashion. We took turns.

As each girl got out of the car, he asked us the same question: "Are you going to have a good day or a GREAT day?"

Every.

Single.

Morning.

Planting seeds of a good day. Seeds of hope. Seeds that helped us understand that it was up to us to determine how we reacted to our day. Every morning he asked us this question, and he was never daunted by the lackluster way we responded. "Are you going to have a good day or a GREAT day?"

"Train up a child in the way he should go, And when he is old he will not depart from it"

(Proverbs 22:6 NKJV).

His morning routine was something I could not comprehend growing up. However, as an adult, I covet and try to emulate it. I work to make my own morning routine my solace. I have found that getting up before the house gets busy to workout, pray, write my list of action items, and read my Bible helps put the priorities in the right order. I don't succeed each morning – my dad did a much better job of being consistent – but I try, hard. Sometimes, just working hard makes you better every day.

"Girls!" I shouted. "We have to go now!" I had 90 minutes...only 90 minutes to get the girls to school! I needed to drive from Coopertown to Springfield and then to Brentwood. This commute typically took 90 minutes on a good day. It was not looking like a good day. Why is it so hard to get two kids in the car? My dad taught us that there should be no decisions made in the morning when you have school-age kids.

Time is precious in the morning. Make all the decisions and do everything you must at night, not in the morning. There is just never enough time.

I had already carried the two lunch boxes to the car, one fiddle, one set of shoes for clogging practice, an extra change of clothes, my coffee and breakfast because I did not take time to eat at home; we needed to leave. I was standing on the stairs, and if I were a dragon, fire would have been coming out of my nose.

"Girls! NOW!!!!!"

I was huffing and puffing, and mad. These mornings would make even the strongest-willed person crumble under the weight of parenthood. We all got into the car, backpacks, laptop case, purse, and football. Yes, a football. An orange football Amelia loves. I am not sure why we had a football, but Amelia, my oldest, wanted to bring it. And I was not happy about it. But to be fair, I was not really happy about anything at that moment. Sometimes, I wonder, if I am ever glad as I look back at these parenting moments. Parenting is hard. How did my dad do it so well or, at least, make it look easy?

And there was a device in the car, breaking the house rule of no devices in the morning. Device, in this case, was an old worn out iPad with a black keyboard cover. The iPad that, if it dropped again, would surely die. If it were a cat, it would be on its 8th life.

I spied the iPad about halfway to school through the rearview mirror. I also discovered that my youngest, Reagan, had smuggled fingernail polish in the car and painted her nails (reasonably okay, I'll have to say) on the way to school. I stopped and got out of the car because I was too mad to keep driving. We were in an abandoned building parking lot on our drive to school. I was going to be late, and again I was fuming.

There must be another way. How did Dad do this? He made it seem easy when it wasn't at all! Or did time make it look smoother than it was?

I dropped the girls off at school and called my dad. I talk to him every morning on my way to work. "Dad, this morning was terrible," I said with a shaky voice on the verge of tears. "Nothing went right. Nothing."

Dad, a great listener, heard and felt every word I said to him, listening the way only a caring parent can. I finally finished telling him how terrible the girls acted. Quite frankly, I was thinking he would reinforce my need to feel validated and side with me about how awful my girls were that morning. But he surprised me by saying, "What can you do to make tomorrow better?" And then, he poured salt further into my wound by saying, "You know it's your responsibility to make the day start out great. *Did you ask them if they were going to have a good day or a GREAT day?"*

I shamefully thought about the morning and how the day went. It was the worst morning we had. Hanging up the phone with Dad, I cried. I cried for the morning I could not get back and for the things I thought and said about the girls. I cried because these are the children I had prayed for and wanted more than anything else in the world. Yet, I did not behave that way.

Dad's strategy was to give us time to get ready while he took the time he needed for himself. I realized I was not doing it the way he did. I did not listen to his advice in totality. I did not set up my morning to be successful. I decided that tomorrow, a new day, I will plant the seeds of a good day for my children. I owe it to them and to myself.

Dad said no decisions should be made in the morning so I packed lunches at night and checked homework and papers. I didn't load the meals in the car or put the backpacks in the car. The best offense is a good defense.

Tomorrow will be different. *Is it going to be a good day or a GREAT day?* I have that power to make it a GREAT day.

"For this child, I prayed, and the LORD has granted me my petition which I asked of Him" (I Samuel 1:27 NKJV).

The next morning was better. I got up earlier and reminded myself that my girls were blessings from God. They were not distractions or impositions. Lunches were packed and neatly set on the bottom shelf of the fridge. Everything that could be in the car was put in the car or by the back door.

We made it to the car, which was still a bit of a process. But there were no tears. On the way to school, the girls got into a bickering conversation. Instead of stopping the car on the road, (a result that only punishes me because it delays me but does not affect the girls at all), I used a trick from a friend. I had a spray bottle filled with water and when the girls started bickering, I gave them one warning then sprayed them with water. They were now in control of the punishment. Neither girl wanted to arrive at school in wet clothes. The bickering stopped.

"Girls, I'm sorry for how I acted yesterday," I said to them in the car, my eyes filling with tears.

I turned around in my blue Ford Fusion to see both of them.

"It's ok," Amelia said quickly as if to dismiss the comment.

"No, it's not ok. Being mean is not ok, ever. You should never allow people who love you to treat you disrespectfully. It's wrong." I said this to them in the car knowing that they may not understand but I did.

"Mom, we know you try hard," Reagan said, in her 4-year-old wisdom.

Dad apologized to me once when he let his anger get the best of him – it was an apology I always remember. He had bought us McDonald's for supper, a treat, and I had spilled two of the drinks on the grey concrete front porch of our house. I can still feel myself in that spot and can see those drinks spilling in slow motion. Two people from our four-person family would not have a soft drink to go with their meals. Not a huge deal when I think of it now, but to a tired parent on a budget, it was a very big deal. And in that moment, knowing we did not have anything else to drink other than water, it was a tough spot for my dad to be in. I had added one more thing to deal with on his already tough day. He scolded me, cussed, and bit his tongue in a way that only those closest to him have seen. That's when he's really angry. I cried, feeling that I had personally made the evening a complete failure.

Later that evening, he apologized. He was sitting in his red, old, comfortable recliner in our living room. I was lying over the arm of the couch, half on the sofa and half off. Alternately, I was reading a book and watching the news with my dad. My sisters had gone to bed. He looked at me with tears in his eyes and with a softness I had never seen before and said, "Donita, I am sorry for getting mad at you today."

He never apologized again for his actions, and he never spoke to me that way ever. His apology was simple. It was straight from his heart. Even at that young middle school age, I felt his apology, and I knew that he meant it. He loved my sisters and me more than anything else. Parenting is hard work.

Dad's apology uniquely shaped my life. It showed me that it's easy to say you are sorry. Saying "sorry" is not just a word; it's a feeling from the heart. It's difficult to mean it and express it from your heart the way my dad did. It's even harder but more rewarding to change your actions because of it. His actions changed from that day. He rarely lost his temper over little things.

"Girls," I said as we got near their school, "are you going to have a good day or a GREAT day?"

"Huh?" Amelia said. "What you do you mean?"

"Amelia, it's up to you to have a good day or a great day; you get to decide each morning how your day is going to go. Are you going to have a good day or a GREAT day!"

"Well, I'm going to have a Supercalifragilis-ticexpialidocious Day!" Reagan said. "I'm going to have a GRRRRRRREAT day," sounding a bit like Tony the Tiger from the Frosted Flake commercials.

Each day since the day of the worst morning ever, I have asked, or, at least, I try to ask the girls if they are going to have a good day or a great day.

They do not always respond "great day," sometimes, it's faked and contrived. Other times, asking them is hard because my heart isn't in it, but I ask them anyway because they get it now, and so do I.

I can start their day out well by how I start my day out.

Part III:
Wisdom from a Caring Parent

Lesson 6

Steak and Boloney

"A dream doesn't become reality through magic; it takes sweat, determination and hard work." - Colin Powell

"I DON'T UNDERSTAND!" I told my dad in frustration. We were sitting at our dining room table, alone. Alone was odd in our house that was usually abuzz with activity. My sisters coming and going or friends stopping by for one reason or another kept the house busy. If those walls could talk, they would laugh at the conversations we had one day and cry for the ones we had on other days.

I was a college student at Austin Peay State University when my dad first shared this next piece of advice with me.

The table we were sitting at was the place for many deep conversations, laughter, and tears. It was the epicenter of our house on Garner Street. My sisters and I ate dinner at this table with Dad, studied our homework and played games such as Phase 10, Triumph and Skip-Bo. We played lots of card games.

The dining room table was significant to our family; it had been my paternal grandparents'. It was the same table my paternal grandfather (as I was told) would tie my baby walker to when he and his wife were eating supper as they babysat me.

My college experience was different from that of many of my high school friends. Austin Peay was in Clarksville, TN and close to Fort Campbell, KY, an Army Base. As a result, this college had many military spouses and non-traditional students. Often, these non-traditional students had spent time in the military. Or they were looking for a second chance at life by getting a degree for a career change. I enjoyed Austin Peay; it was challenging and valued education.

I was lamenting about a "friend" – well, really someone I just knew. The person was driving a brand new car and had a great job right out of high school. However, I was commuting back-and-forth each day to college. It didn't seem fair. I was angry about it and was talking about how unfair it was to my dad. As I reminisce, I find myself embarrassed at the entire interaction. Dad worked tirelessly to provide for my sisters and me, on his own, without a helpmate. Yet, I dared to complain about life not being fair.

I could not wrap my head around why I was doing all this hard work when this person I knew was able to land a job and make more money than me even when I graduated from college with a degree. I was commuting to school; a 45-minute drive each way. I could not afford to live on campus. It felt so frustrating to see other people I knew from high school taking what seemed to be the easy way out.

I was studying at that dining room table. My typical schedule was to study all morning Saturday and Sunday. My boyfriend, now husband and I had study dates on Saturday nights and all day Sunday. I studied alone on Saturday morning. During the week I also had, at least, one job, sometimes two – all while going to college full time.

This Saturday morning's study session was part of my regular routine and almost a solace. I studied on Saturday morning because it seemed like it took me twice as long as everyone else to study. I doubted any of my peers were studying as much as I was. Interestingly enough, this time, I was living the advice Dad had yet to give me. I didn't mind studying but when I compared myself to someone else I knew wasn't doing so on a Saturday, I was mad. Comparison stole my joy.

"There are two things you are going to eat in life, steak, and boloney; you get to choose the order," my dad explained to me. He continued, "You can eat your steak now and then later, you will get to eat baloney. Or you can eat your baloney now and eat your steak later."

I was waiting tables at a Ponderosa at nights, working at a travel agency 2 days a week, going to school 3 days a week and on the weekend working at a Radio Shack. *Life just seemed hard. However, hard wasn't really what it was.*

I had the opportunity to go to school, to college. I see the opportunity now but I didn't then. Some people never go to college. My yoke (going to school) was my privilege. And I was wearing it proudly. I had dug into it. Wearing it like a badge of honor.

My dad told me when I graduated high school that he could not afford to send me to college. However, he could afford to let me live at home, provide my food, and wash my clothes. That was a deal in hindsight. I wish I had been more appreciative of it then.

Most days were something like this: Tuesdays and Thursdays, I had arranged to have all my classes and would leave the house before 7:00 AM. I would drive an hour to Clarksville Tennessee to the campus of Austin Peay State University, take classes until however late I needed, most times, 4:00 or 5:00 PM, drive another hour home and then help my dad with whatever I could in the evenings.

Mondays, Wednesdays, and Fridays, I worked in a travel agency from 8:00 AM to 5:00 PM. After 5:00 PM, I waited tables at Ponderosa. On weekends, I worked at Radio Shack in Springfield.

I learned a lot about people both as workers and customers working in a restaurant. It was disheartening to see how customers treated workers who did what could be perceived as trivial tasks. Working with adults who had chosen this profession made me strive not to work in that area for the rest of my life. Being a professional cook or waitress was hard on the body and the pay at this type of restaurant was not sustainable for me long-term.

"Right now, you are eating your baloney, but one day, you will get to eat your steak. Be patient, the best is yet to come." **Steak or Baloney**? I was never content with what I had, always wanting more and finding a way to get it. Eating my boloney, but really craving my steak. I didn't know that boloney didn't taste good until I saw someone else eating their steak. Comparing yourself to others is the thief of joy.

Contentment is what my dad was trying to teach me. Power is in learning to love where you are in life. Finding the good. And there is always good.

"Not that I am speaking of being in need, for I have learned in whatever situation I am to be content" (Philippians 4:11, ESV).

I haven't arrived yet, and I probably won't ever arrive. Steak or baloney is a mindset. It's choosing to do the hard things when everyone else is taking the easy way out. My oldest daughter, Amelia, made a bad decision in 4th grade. She chose the steak. She had a book report to turn in.

In her class, they had one book to read over a two-week period with a very well thought out timeline by her teacher. They had a date to turn in the rough draft and one to turn in the final draft. The final draft was to be copied from the rough draft.

Amelia thought it would be "ok" not do the hard work; rather, she would just take the rough draft, erase the words "rough draft" and turn it in for the final copy. *Why would you do extra work, as the teacher required, when you could take a shortcut?* she validated in her mind. This was the equivalent of eating your steak first instead of the baloney. Her teacher recognized the infraction and called me one Friday night. "Amelia," her Dad said to her, "what you did was not right and now you will have to do more work to make up for not doing it right the first time." She had to eat her baloney anyway. **There are two things in life you will eat: steak and baloney; you get to choose the order.** Amelia's punishment was to do another book report, from a different book and turn it into us, her parents.

I'm still working hard and heeding this advice every day. I have a fantastic job, boss, home, and family.   Honestly, life is excellent.   But there can always be more.   Do more for others and be more of a positive example every day.   I keep a post-it note on my desk, written when I started with the company I am with today, which reads: "There are a thousand people who would like your job; don't waste it."   It's vital for me to remember what a blessing each day is. I must not waste it and keep eating the baloney.

I may not be crying at the kitchen table anymore because life just doesn't seem fair but I also don't need to be eating steak every day. My dad's advice was very poetic when he gave it to me, and it's still relevant today.

Lesson 7

Relationships Are Like an ATM

"Never above you. Never below you. Always beside you." -
Walter Winchell

"MY FLIGHT IS DELAYED," Robert told me. I really didn't want to take his call. The phone woke me up from dozing on the couch in our upstairs family room. This is the room where we spend lazy weekends. Amelia, Reagan, and I were upstairs, watching TV, or instead, they were, and I was trying to rest my eyes, which is code for taking a nap. I was exhausted from the week of doing it all myself with the girls. Thankfully, it was Friday night. We had made it through a week without him being home.

That week was hard. Robert left early Monday and was scheduled to be back late the night he called, Friday. However, plans changed on him. He wouldn't be home as expected. Plans change or, at least, they do if you travel long enough. Travel has so many variables, especially air travel. Although it works as planned most of the time, there are occasions when it does not. That's when the traveler is at the mercy of the airline. It's a sick feeling not knowing when or if you will get home as planned.

"I'm sorry," I told him. "It's terrible to be gone all week and then have this happen." "This," meaning you are ready to go home after giving all you had to your job for the week, and then something happens to prevent you from going home. In this instance, my husband's flight was delayed because of a mechanical issue with the plane. It can be so discouraging. I know, because it has happened to me on more than one occasion.

I went to Utah to work for a week when the last leg of my flight was canceled. My flight out of Salt Lake City was delayed, and so I missed my connection in Dallas by minutes. I got to the gate, but they had closed the door. I know that sick feeling of wanting to be home but not being able to be there because of a canceled flight. My heart was heavy for Robert, my husband, who was in a similar plight.

We are a team. Robert and me. Married for almost 18 years. When an MVP on your team is gone, it's hard for the rest of the team. And that's the way I felt that week. I was down a man, and it's hard when you don't have all your players.

I got up from the couch and walked down the stairs. Careful not to fall, I was really sleepy, but the nap had helped. "I should have taken the voucher," Robert told me, "but I really wanted to be home tonight." He recounted the story of what happened just a few minutes earlier in the terminal. Delta was offering a $600 travel voucher to be used within 12 months for anyone who would like to take a flight the next day. Robert didn't take the coupon. In hindsight, he should have, because the plane was canceled anyway. Had he taken the ticket, he would have gotten a free flight for us to use later in the year, plus, he would have arrived at a hotel much sooner than he eventually did that night.

I was thoroughly awake when I walked down the steps. And I was glad I took Robert's call. He was lonely at the airport and that's a terrible feeling. It was loud in the background. I could hear the overhead over the phone announcing other flights leaving the terminal; it was almost as if they were mocking us. Flights were departing but not Robert's.

The girls and I had already talked to him once that night while we were eating supper. He was glad to be at the airport and ready to be home – now, this delay made it worse; we were so excited that we would see him soon and more than ready for him to be back.

"Donita, relationships are like an ATM. You can't expect to cash in without already having a deposit in the bank."

Remembering this sage advice, from my dad, I kept talking to Robert – when really, all I wanted to do was sleep. When there is only one person at home with two kids, the time goes by too quickly. There's much to do at night when we get home from school and work. There is homework, supper, baths, packing lunches, practicing clogging and fiddle, and housework. That day I had gone with Reagan's class to the zoo for their fall field trip.

Robert and I talked for about thirty more minutes. We discussed each day he was gone and most nights we Face-Timed for the girls to see him. It was hard. When we spoke during the week, I was not very friendly. I was tired, overwhelmed, and missed my husband. I rarely had a free moment at night and as I was the only parent home, we were typically an hour later getting in bed than usual.

Relationships are like an ATM. You can't expect to cash in without already having a deposit in the bank.

I don't remember when my dad first said those words to me. I remember several instances where he used this advice but I can't recall the first time he said it. It was almost as if the help was always there. This lesson, about filling up one's relationship bank, was something Dad lived.

Now, as adults, we fill each other's relationship banks by talking on the phone on our way to work. He enjoys hearing about the daily activities of my daughters. And I enjoy listening to him talk about his day.

Filling someone's relationship bank isn't just a nice thing to do. If you are in a relationship, it's mandatory. Each person's need is different based on their wants, desires, and personalities. Some people prefer time; others want gifts. The key to success is knowing what fulfills the person.

The Five Love Languages by Gary Chapman is the best source for finding your partner's needs and yours but it isn't just for couples. In Chapman's book, he defines each of the Love Languages and provides a quiz on how to determine your love language. According to Chapman, they are Words of Affirmation, Quality Time, Receiving Gifts, Acts of Service, and Physical Touch. Nothing is magical about these love languages and like much advice, it seems pretty essential; however, it isn't always easy to implement. Often, we think and act in ways that make us happy, not necessarily the other person in the relationship.

As said earlier, the love languages in Chapman's book will help you determine your partner's needs and yours. However, it doesn't stop there. There are love languages for work and children, as well as the original for couples. Simply put, the love languages are Words of Affirmation (telling someone they are doing a good job or that we appreciate them), Quality Time (spending time with them), Receiving Gifts (buying them meaningful presents), Acts of Services (doing tasks for others) and Physical Touch (a pat on the arm or a hug).

We tend to focus a lot on couples' relationships. However, filling relationship banks is also crucial for parents and children, friend groups, and co-workers. If you ever want to find out why there is a strain between two people, take a look at their relationship bank – it's probably low.

During the Christmas season, my daughters, my friend Naomi and I went to the Christmas Sampler in Springfield at the Center. In its 39th year, it's a mandatory event if you are a resident of Robertson County. Indeed, it's not a required function but it does seem that way. This event is a collaboration between all the women's clubs in Robertson County. It's the kick off of the holiday season in our small town. It is a good old-fashion craft show held the first weekend of November annually. Each year the same vendors are there. It's an ideal place to buy Christmas presents, and most importantly, to see people you haven't seen since last year at the Sampler. I've had many conversations which started, "How are your parents?" Or asking someone, I saw at the Sampler how their kids were doing.

I doubted the wisdom in taking Reagan, my youngest, to the Sampler on that Friday night. Amelia, my oldest, thrives in places with lots of people and action. Reagan is an introvert, and conversely, Amelia is an extrovert. While some may doubt my labeling of my daughters at such a young age, 7 and 9, I know that's what they are and how to fill their banks. But I failed this time.

Amelia loves life and has two primary speeds, which are awake and asleep. Everything is exciting to her. She loves everyone and everything. Reagan, as an introvert, has many different speeds. One of which is going home on Friday nights and being only with family, preferably watching TV while cuddling with her dad or me. She doesn't love doing things on Friday nights, and typically it ends poorly when we try.

I picked my daughters up from school and asked them if they wanted to go. Amelia responded with a resounding, "yes!" And Reagan said, "sure" timidly. I asked a few probing questions about their days, grabbed Reagan's hand, bent down close to her, and asked her if she would rather have her daddy come pick her up so she didn't have to go. Not wanting to be left out, she assured me she wanted to go. I was not convinced that it was a good idea but I took her anyway.

It wasn't a good idea.

Friday nights, the Sampler opens at 4:00 PM and runs until 9:00 PM. Saturday, it is open from 8:30 AM to 5:00 PM. Before we got there, we needed food. A quick supper at our favorite fast food stop, Sonic. Then we were off to pick up Naomi. Parking at the Sampler can be problematic and there was no need for Naomi to drive. I was happy to spend a few extra minutes together with her in the car, picking her up and taking her home afterward.

Naomi and her husband Bill had just returned from a Habit for Humanity House built in Central America only two days before our trek to the Sampler. Naomi's love language is giving gifts. I know this because when I walk into her home where she has lived for 20+ years, her kitchen table is lined with handmade gifts brought back from her trip.

She carefully and thoughtfully purchased them with the intent to give each to a specific person. She bought a gift for me, my two daughters, my two sisters, my mom, and my dad. There were more than thirty gifts on the table, and she told me who each was for, where and why she purchased it.

After we parked my car, we proceeded to the door of the Sampler and purchased our tickets. The tickets provided an entry to both Friday and Saturday's events. They were also your tickets to the raffle; typically, the prize is a quilt or something similar.

Two folding tables were set up at the point where you could buy your tickets. Many people were milling around, and immediately, Reagan hid her face in my shirt. There were too many people for her, and her relationship bank was low. She wanted to be with me and go to the Sampler, but this was a mistake.

We walked in and went to the first booth. Then her small voice asked me if I would carry her. I know she needed to be held close before she got comfortable around all the people there. On the other hand, Amelia was excited and couldn't wait to see all there was to see. She had a listing of all the vendors, and at the third booth, she saw something she wanted to buy for her 4th-grade teacher, Miss Hart.

"Amelia, we have to go to all the booths before we make a purchase. That's our rule for tonight. Write on your list what you want from each booth, and once we have been to all of them, we will go back and decide what we are going to get."

Amelia nodded that she understood and quickly began to mark the booths off and made her plans on what to purchase. Before we arrived at the Sampler, I told the girls we were only buying Christmas presents for other people. That's it. We were not buying toys or gifts for ourselves.

Amelia was on a mission the rest of the evening to mark off all the booths so that later, she could buy her presents for those on her list. Reagan spent the rest of the night either being carried, cranky, or riding on my back.

I realized that going to the Sampler filled Naomi and Amelia's relationship bank. They both appreciated the time. While Naomi's love language is gifts, she also appreciates spending time with others. Amelia's love language is quality time, and we spent plenty of time together that evening. However, I depleted Reagan's relationship bank. She was worn out from school and our night together with the rest of Robertson County did nothing to fill that bank.

Relationships are like an ATM. You can't expect to cash in without already having a deposit in the bank.

This week Dad called me, after our daily call in the evening. A call back from Dad usually signifies one of two things: he forgot to tell me something, or there was something wrong. "Donita," he said, and I immediately knew something was wrong. "What's wrong?" I asked, a little uneasy. "Oh, my low-pressure warning for one of my tires is on, and I don't want to drive an hour on it. Could I borrow one of your vehicles?" Well, he could, but Robert was out of town, and the "other" vehicle was at the airport. "Dad, I am so sorry but the other car is at the airport." Dad just sighed. I knew he was exasperated and tired.

Dad had left work late, doing some catch-up work and all the local automotive places in town were closed. "Let me call you back," he said. "I'm going to put air in the tire and see if that fixes it."

His office was undergoing some construction, and he had a pretty good idea that he had picked up a nail in his tire. My dad's commute was an hour home, and he knew it wasn't wise to drive on a tire that had a nail in it.

I was almost home; it was late evening, and the traffic had been smooth so far that night. I was running ideas through my mind, trying to figure out how I could help Dad. The "new" Wal-Mart in town, the one built more than ten years ago, but still "new" to those of us who are Springfield natives, has an automotive department.

I called the number for the store, and a woman with a pleasant voice greeted me, asking how she could help, "Automotive department," I said, pleased with my idea.

"Auto," the guy said.

"Hello, how late are you open tonight?" I asked.

"7 PM," he replied.

Fabulous! It was 5:30 pm.

Promptly, I called Dad back but he didn't sound any better.

"Hey," I said. "Wal-mart is open until 7:00 PM, and they have an automotive department," I told him. "They can fix your tire, and you can get on your way."

"Oh, that's great," he said. "I'm headed there now, thank you."

I hung up with him and called my sister, Danielle. I relayed the story and told her I was thinking about stopping by to see him at Wal-Mart to brighten his day. She encouraged me to do so. I was tired. Ready to go home but I knew it would make his day a little brighter. This small act of kindness cost me a candy bar, which I bought for him on my way to get my daughters at school.

I picked up my girls and told them we were going to Wal-Mart. They were excited; we never stopped there during the week because it takes every moment to get home, get supper, and do homework. So that night, we were a little later getting to bed. We needed to make a deposit into the relationship ATM.

I called Dad when we got to Wal-Mart.

"Where are you?" I asked him.

"Oh, I'm walking around the store; figured I could get some steps in while I'm waiting. I just told Barbara I was going to be late, guess supper will wait." My dad walks every day. He walks in the morning, he walks at lunchtime, and he walks in the evenings. It's his solace. He rarely ends his day without 15,000 steps registering on his Fitbit. I wish my activity diligence were the same as his. But he and I are in different seasons of life. This is what is necessary for him now.

Barbara was waiting for him at home. She is the love of his life and his second wife, my step-mother. This is the wife he waited many years to find. She is the one I'm sure he thought might have never come. They are an excellent fit for each other. While both are introverts, their personalities are different enough to complement one another. They both love to go on weekend adventures. Often, their weekends consist of road trips, picnics, and long walks together.

"Pappy!" My daughters shouted when they saw him. We had just turned down the aisle and spied him with his back turned, wearing his red rain jacket. He was still wearing his work clothes: khaki pants, and a polo shirt. He smiled. I was glad I came. I offered him a hug and gave him a candy bar. He laughed and told me that the candy bar would be a sweet treat to have on the way home. Hugging him was good. He seemed to need the hug.

We looked at the bicycles that were close to the automotive department. Reagan, my youngest daughter needed a new one, as she finally started to grow a little. In less than twenty minutes, Dad's name was called overhead, signifying that his car was ready. We all walked back to the auto department and were relieved to find out there was no nail in his tire. Each tire had been carefully checked and aired up. Dad was on his way.

Dad reached for his wallet and took out five one dollar bills. He offered them to the mechanic and said, "thank you." There was no charge for the work since there was really no work done.

Nevertheless, Dad wanted to pay into the relationship ATM bank of this guy – something my dad often does to strangers; he selflessly gives to others. Random acts of kindness like this fill his relationship bank to the world. He wanted to give this guy a tip as a way of saying thank you.

The store's policy prohibited the man from taking the money, but Dad's kind gesture was not wasted as the man's face softened, and he smiled.

Lesson 8

There Will Always Be Someone Better Than You

"Don't tell me the sky's the limit when there are footprints on the moon." - Paul Brandt

"DAD, I DIDN'T GET FIRST CHAIR," I said, crying, as I walked into the house. I started crying as I pulled into the driveway in my beloved 1968 Brittany Blue Mustang. The driveway between our house and the next house was my permanent parking spot. My dad, the only other driver at the time in our house always parked at the front of the house. I parked in the driveway. I'm not sure why it was this way but it was. If the light pole on the corner of our lot could talk it would tell of the many times I pulled into the driveway on two wheels. This time, it saw me pull into my parking spot barely making it to the house before I started crying. I took a deep breath, reached for the handle of the car, purposefully opened the door and with the next breath, I started crying. A soft cry at first then a body shaking cry when I made it into the house.

The Mustang was my dream car. I not only loved it but also held my breath every time I drove it. I wasn't sure if it would take me where I needed to go; it was always a roll of the dice if we would make it to my final destination. It ran... the majority of the time. But not always. I always took a little risk taking it anywhere but what is life without a bit of risk?

The car was not comfortable to ride in or drive but it was cool. Being a lover of old cars, this vehicle was heavenly to me despite the creature comforts it lacked. It had no air conditioning and the hand-cranked windows that required a lot of muscle were hard to roll down. But who really needs air in the south in the summer? A car should get you to where you are going but this car was unique, and even when occasionally it didn't deliver me to my destination, I still loved it.

Its original color "Brittany Blue" meant that at one time it had been this color. The years had oxidized the paint, and it was now more of an "at one time – Brittany Blue" color. Rust was visible on certain areas of the car. The interior was battered and worn. What was once a vinyl seat was now a seat with a towel thrown over it because the seats were tattered and torn from years of sunlight. The car was loud and there was no denying when it was on the road. It was LOUD.

Much like a person who lacked care, this car showed the years of neglect. I didn't really care how it looked, inside or out, as long as it was a Mustang – my then car obsession. Obsession because it was different, just like I was, a little different. It was mine – paid for with my own earnings from my various jobs.

My Big Papaw was the epitome of the southern gentleman. I never saw him outside his house in East Tennessee home when he didn't have a hat and a jacket. A true southern gentleman in the 1990s always wore a hat. It was as if wearing a hat was a requirement for good manners.

John Sidney Cox was born in 1913; he lived through the Great Depression. I loved this man more than anything when I was a kid. He was tall, strong, and could cook – a trait he passed along to his son, my Little Papaw, who was my mom's dad. He and my Mamaw were who I called my grandparents, but in reality, they were my great-grandparents. It got confusing to explain this, so I rarely did. After all, who really wants to know the deep secrets about your family drama? In reality, no one.

I told my Big Pawpaw how much I liked Mustangs when I was 15; I was obsessed with them. I had every Mustang book that had been published and frequently bought Mustang magazines when I could. So being a good grandfather, he found one for me to buy when I was ready to purchase a car. However, there was a catch. The guy he wanted to buy it from didn't sell cars to women. This gentleman had sold a car to a female, the only one he had ever sold to a lady; she wrecked it and died in the accident. From that day on, he decided he would never sell another car to a woman.

The man officially sold the car to my dad who then signed it over to me. Purchased for $1,200 of hard earned money and bought on a loan that my dad co-signed for me from our local credit union.

If this car had been a person, it would have been my best friend. When I was lonely or needed to be someplace important, it carried me to my destination. It was almost like it knew when to break down and did so at the times that were perfect, allowing me time to be alone with my thoughts. It was almost human and often felt that way. The car and I had a connection that was started in love with my Big Papaw.

The car had been given its nickname by my friends from high school. We all had nicknames in high school among the group of friends I hung out with. And the car with so much personality just fit in. The "Wustang" was aptly named because the "M" on the"MUSTANG" on the trunk was broken and hung sideways, making the "M" look like a "W."

My car had style.

A few spots of rust on it and a few places of Bondo. In truth, it needed a complete restoration, and it required the type of person who could give such a beautiful car just that. But for that time, we had a good relationship, the Wustang and I. I took as good care of her as I was able to, and – most of the time – she took me where I needed to go.

That day, I was thankful that my car helped me get home and did not betray me. Her seats welcomed me when I climbed into her after seeing the list that did not have my name as first chair trumpet. I was second chair. Second, not first.

Second best, after trying my hardest. My best was not good enough. And my best was all I had to give. I sunk into the seat, rolled down the driver's window, and leaned across to roll down the passenger window. It was a hot day as most days in August in Tennessee and my beloved Mustang had no air conditioning.

I held it together when I saw the list hung up on the door of the band room after school. I shrugged it off as if second chair would be ok. With several people around, I told those who could hear me, I was glad not to have the pressure of being the first chair. In fact, it was a complete waste of time to have to be the top. Of course, I was lying. I desperately wanted to play first chair trumpet. The auditions for our band had been earlier that day, and I just knew I had played my absolute best.

But my best wasn't good enough. And this time, on this day, it was ok. Dad had a valuable life lesson to teach me on such a challenging day.

Dad was busy in the kitchen ironing. He ironed all his clothes on his day off, which some years was Wednesdays and others it was another day of the week. However, this year it was Wednesday and he has masterfully ironing on this Wednesday. No one could use an iron like my dad.

He liked the way the creases looked on his pants, and it must have been relaxing for him to iron because he did it so methodically. He had a rhythm to using the iron, one that neither my sisters nor I could ever master. In fact, now, as an adult, I don't even own an iron – that iron has defeated me. If anything needs wrinkles removed, I steam it or take it to a dry cleaner. But there's something very relaxing about watching my dad iron. Everything he does, as always, is done in an order that makes perfect sense.

You had to be careful walking in the kitchen where he ironed because he always stood in the same place and sprayed Fantastic Spray Starch on his clothes as he ironed them. The yellow-topped can still stayed on top of the fridge. Always the yellow-topped aerosol can, never any other type or brand. The spray starch, from years of spraying, had created a slick spot on the floor. If you hit it just right, you'd slip and fall! Just ask my sister, Danielle, she fell many times in this spot, a victim of the slick place.

At that time, I was a junior in high school. One more year left of what were supposed to be the wonder years of high school. A lot of my personal pride and who I was hung on my getting the first chair in the Springfield Marching Band. In reality, my own satisfaction and who I was, were and have always been rooted in my accomplishments. Not things, thank goodness because my car was a testament to the fact that I didn't care as much about worldly things as I did about experiences and achievements.

I played the trumpet; an instrument I picked because few women played this instrument and the one female I once saw play it looked fierce. I wanted to be fierce. To be the tough gal in class and to go against the grain. I never relied on being cool or doing the same as everyone else. But I also wasn't so different that I was a rebel. I was just my own self.

"Dad, I tried so hard," I said, crying even harder now. He stepped out from behind the ironing board and moved toward me. He made a deliberate move to turn off the iron then he unplugged it. He was intentional in his actions. He put his arms around my shoulders, and I buried my head in his chest. We were still standing in the kitchen. "Let's sit on the front porch," he said. He didn't have time to just sit on the front porch but he always knew when he needed to make time. He had the gift that few do to make you feel as if you were the only thing that mattered when he spoke to you and this time was no different.

Our front porch swing was the center of the social scene at my house. My friends and my sisters' friends hung out on our front porch whenever we could. Our porch was big enough to fit several friends in the wicker seats and the white porch swing that decorated it. The porch gave us the comfort of our home, the freedom, and space to spend time with our friends. It was an inviting place to be, where time seemed to linger and go at a slower pace.

Outside our house, on a sleepy street in the historic district of Springfield, was just as inviting as the front porch itself. The road rarely saw any-thing terrible; there wasn't any crime to speak of on this street. During the time I lived there, there were a couple of car break-ins, which were the talk of the block and many cars that drove too fast but that was the extent of the excitement there.

Most of the people who lived on this street were older, and the road had an excellent slower-paced vibe to it. It was also lined with large trees that welcomed you as you walked or drove down the road. In the spring and autumn, the road was the prettiest in the city as the trees changed colors.

Our porch swing was something to be wit-nessed. It was shiny white with many coats of paint and had somehow weathered the years well, unlike our porch, which showed its age. The swing was hung from the ceiling of the porch on two sizeable red tractor springs. These springs, if you weren't aware of them before sitting on the swing, gave the sitter a surprise. Regular porch swings don't have a "give" in them, but this porch swing, hung on those tractor springs, had a gentle comfortable sway to it, making the experience even more inviting. There were also two small couch pillows on the swing that fitted nicely on your back.

And on that hot August day, my sweet dad, the man I knew always loved me no matter what looked at me with a softness in his eyes that I rarely had the opportunity to see. His face was usually filled with expressions that reflected his task list, as his thoughts moved from one thing to the next in his efforts to take care of his family. The daily stresses built lines on his forehead which, if they could talk, would each have a story to tell about each of his daughters and the joys and sorrows we caused.

"Donita, **there will always be someone better than you**," he said. We were sitting on the porch swing and Dad had his arm around me. I was taken aback by his statement and frankly, a little put off. I just looked at him.

"You can't be good in everything," he went on to say. "You got to figure out what you can do, and then just do it well."

This lesson stung. What I didn't understand was that the lesson wasn't over. I had to learn more about this wisdom, and I wouldn't learn it all until many years later.

"There will always be someone better than you."

No matter what we do in life, there will always be someone better. The quest in life is to pick those things that are important enough to accomplish and then work as hard as you can.

While I've often weighed my worth internally by my accomplishments, today, this lesson also reminds me not to take myself too seriously. There is more to life than these achievements. Alone we can go fast, but if we choose to go together, with others, we can go farther in life.

While this advice *that there will always be someone better than you* does sting, it also gives me comfort to remember that we aren't in this life alone. Once you accept this piece of advice, it allows you to see those who are better than you and to learn from them.

"Therefore encourage one another and build one another up, just as you are doing" (1 Thessalonians 5:11 ESV).

I've learned this lesson a few times recently with my children. The first time, was at the end of the school year awards ceremony. Most parents know these awards ceremonies well. I would bet they are almost all the same. Both the students and parents seemed nervous.

The first time this lesson rang true to me was when my daughters, Reagan and Amelia, were in kindergarten and 3rd grade. I think back to my oldest daughter's first awards ceremony, her kindergarten year. That year, she won so many awards. She was elated and proudly displayed those awards in her room. Each year since then, the awards have gotten fewer for her. Each year is harder as it should be.

Last year's ceremony resulted in Amelia crying as we walked out. This year, I was not sure how it was going to go. As the names were announced for each of the awards, I watched her face fall when her name wasn't called. This year was much like the last. She was so disappointed she didn't get the math award, her best subject. She gave it her all but it wasn't enough. I know that feeling.

As we walked out of the school, she was teary. It was not the time to have the discussion. I let her be with her feelings. It's tough to be so young and want life to be fair. But fair isn't the real world.

There will always be someone better than you.

Lesson 8

Continued: There Will Always Be Someone Better Than You

"It takes a wise man to learn from his mistakes, but an even wiser man to learn from others." - Zen Proverb

BOTH MY DAUGHTERS COMPETE IN

Bluegrass Festivals. Amelia, my oldest, competes in dancing and Reagan, my youngest, competes in the fiddle. It's a fiddle, not a violin. There's nothing wrong with playing the violin, but that's not what my daughter plays.

Sure, it's technically the same instrument but there's a world of difference in how you play these two, and it's really all about attitude. My youngest has plenty of attitude, so she plays the fiddle.

These Bluegrass Festivals can be found all around the country. We are fortunate in Middle Tennessee, where we live, to be within driving distance of many of the great festivals. Some of the great include Smithville Fiddler's Jamboree in Smithville, TN, Tennessee Valley Fiddler's Convention in Athens, AL, and 1890's Day Jamboree in Ringgold, GA. At each of these events, there are multiple bluegrass competitions for musicians and dancers.

These are fun events, and as a family, we enjoy them. Some families spend their time at a ball field; we choose to spend our weekends at Blue-grass Festivals.

We first chose to be Bluegrass Festival goers when Amelia, my oldest, showed an interested in clogging at the age of five. She was taking ballet and hated it. As in – cried each week. It was not her pace as she was a five-year-old with an extra dose of God-given energy. She loved the outfit she got to wear in ballet and truth be told, that's why she liked the first week. But the movements in ballet didn't fit her personality. Her ballet class was up a wooden staircase in the dance studio situated in downtown Springfield, our hometown.

The dance studio's name was "Main Stage," set aptly on Main Street in Springfield with the hope of training dancers and musicians to become entertainers who would one day perform on the main stage.

Amelia was in tears as we left her class one day – she was not enjoying her thirty-minute ballet lesson. We walked by the clogging class at the same dance studio. She stopped dead in her tracks; she was mesmerized. She could not stop

watching the girls dancing with their white clogging shoes that make an excellent loud clackety-
clack and the girls dancing to upbeat bluegrass
music – they were clogging! She fell in love with
this style of dancing. It spoke to her soul. That
day sealed the deal for Amelia; from that point on,
she was a clogger.

Each year, she has gotten a little better dancing and competing. This year, at the age of nine,
she's outstanding, but out of the 15 competitions
we have been to, she has only placed in one. Just
as my dad's advice reminds me of the lesson I
learned in high school, *there will always be someone better than you.* Reagan has just started
competing with the fiddle and dances occasionally.   Much like her sister, each time she
competes she gets a little better.

Each competition has its own personality.
Some of the festivals are laid back, like the towns
where they are located and some are not. However, in each competition, the person competing
in the event is the focus of the show and for a few
minutes, the stage is hers. The first time Reagan

competed with her fiddle, she was four and a pre-schooler. We were at a competition in Clarksville, TN, the one that we could consider to be the first of our Bluegrass Festival season. The festival is indoors, thankfully, as it was February and cold. This is the only indoor festival we attend. The stage is enormous, especially for a four-year-old. Actually, it was huge to me, too. Just looking at the stage made my heart skip a beat. I do not let on that I think the stage is big. We were there last year for Amelia to dance and Reagan was playing in the back, not paying attention as she was only three.

What a difference a year makes.

One year later, Reagan, was standing on that stage.

Reagan stood on the stage. Her small fiddle in her hand. She was without her teacher, a safety net for me but not for Reagan. I watched a vital part of her personality form. It was the part where when she made her mind up to do something she would succeed. She didn't have the drive yet to place in the competition but knowing that she could stand on the stage and play a song without getting nervous or backing out was a feat by itself.

What a difference a year makes.

Not having her teacher did not seem to matter to her. She had decided she was going to play and play she did. My husband was able to find someone backstage to "back her up" for her little song that she had planned to play. This "backing her up" was a concept that was foreign to me until Reagan started to play the fiddle and compete.

Each musician needs someone to play an instrument that complements his/her music. With the fiddle, typically, there is a person who plays accompaniment on a guitar. This person generally is the teacher for some students, or for others, it is the best guitar player you can find.

Most people at these festivals just love to play and never mind backing up someone they may later compete against or may not have ever met. The spirit of the competition is something that is unique to only these events.

Yes, it's a competition. But the musicians also display a willingness to help each other, even those they compete against.

That festival, the one where Reagan stood on the stage and played her little fiddle was three years ago. Now, this weekend we traveled several hours for Amelia and Reagan to compete at the Tennessee Valley Old Time Fiddler's Convention in Athens, Alabama. Amelia planned to compete in dancing and Reagan in Beginning Fiddler.

Amelia is very good at clogging, says her mother, so I am apparently not unbiased. And more importantly, she still enjoys it after 4 years of dancing, which is pretty amazing. We had a brief six-month stint when she took gymnastics instead of clogging but clogging just has her heart.

Amelia's body is built like a dancer. She has long thin but muscular legs, a slim body, and she looks alive when she dances. There are three types of mountain dancing – clogging, buck dancing, and flat foot.

Clogging is an expressive form of dancing, with the dancer wearing clogging shoes, which are similar to tap shoes. These shoes have metal taps on the bottom and are typically black or white. The dancer does steps such as double step, where she is standing on one foot and strikes her other foot twice from toe to heel, in a quick motion. Watching the dancers, you wouldn't even know they were doing it twice. There are other steps that a clogger may typically do when dancing, such as rock step, crazy legs, or heel walks. These dancers are fun to watch, and these competitions tend to draw the most massive crowds of all the events of the day. There are other events besides dancing at these festivals, such as Fiddle, Guitar, Banjo, and Old Time Band. Bluegrass Festivals group the dancers by age. A standard grouping would be aged 10 and under, 11 to 17, 18 to 35, 36 and above, with many variations of these age categories.

Buck Dancing is similar to clogging, but the dancer keeps their upper body still, and there are no high steps or sidekicks, as allowed in clogging competitions. Buck dancing is a little more reserved, with more focus on the technical parts of dancing and not on the showmanship of the dancing.

Flat foot dancing is where the dancer only picks up her feet less than an inch off the ground.

And there is no movement of the upper body. Each of these is set to old-time bluegrass music with a band playing a short song for each competition.

If you compared Clogging to Buck Dancing and Flat Footing – flat foot dancing has the least amount of movement, buck dancing has a little more, and then clogging is the most expressive. It's similar to comparing a canoe to a fishing boat to a speedboat. They are all boats, but with different speeds.

We were told by a fellow Bluegrass Festival goer that the Tennessee Valley Old Time Fiddlers Convention is a good one to attend. However, we realized it is much bigger than we had anticipated. Much bigger. In fact, it might have been the most significant competition we traveled to thus far in our short four years of going to competitions.

We were also in for another surprise at the competition. We found out while registering the girls that Amelia's dance competition was not a clogging competition. Instead, the event was listed as a buck dancing competition. However, after reading the rules for the event, we realized it was really a flat foot competition. These are very different events. Rarely do young dancers compete in flat foot dancing; it's hard and to get it right, you need a lot of experience. It's hard to move to the music and keep your feet less than an inch from the floor. After a small meltdown with tears, Amelia was ready to compete. Well sorta.

We walked around the Bluegrass Festival; it was a beautiful Saturday, October day. The weather forecast had initially called for rain all day, then just rain in the afternoon. Instead, the day turned out quite lovely. It was warm, which is a gift for October but not so hot that it was uncomfortable. The trees still had most of their leaves, and they gave us some welcome shade.

One of the best parts of these festivals is the little jam sessions all around the event. The jam session is where a group of musicians get together and play. Jam sessions at these events are frequent; in almost any shady spot, you'll find a few fiddles, guitars, banjo, and maybe a bass with a singer belting out a bluegrass song. At some of these jams, there are plywood boards set down for people to come up and dance, any style.

We saw a jam session with two plywood boards for dancing – clogging, buck dancing, or flat-footing – you pick. I leaned over to Amelia and told her to go dance. Shyly, she did. Immediately, I saw her face lighting up. She was in her element. Dancing, what she loves to do. She was wearing her street clothes and tennis shoes; she didn't even have her clogging shoes on, but it was just a pickup dance, not the competition – it was just for fun.

Jason Wade, a clogger we love to watch at festivals and one of the greats of clogging whom we have seen many times came over to watch Amelia dance. He was dressed in a long-sleeved button-down red shirt and starched jeans, Wranglers. He looked like a modern-day cowboy. He had a pack of cigarettes in his shirt pocket, and he was wearing a cowboy hat.

He told Amelia what a good job she was doing dancing in a jam. He also told her that the way she was dancing would get her disqualified from the event she had entered. He told us that this event was the strictest for dancers and musicians. "You'll never compete anywhere that's as strict as here in Athens," he said to Robert and me. Jason showed her which moves she could do and for several songs helped her learn the steps she needed for flat foot dancing.

At these competitions, there is a unique community of people who enjoy being together and want each other to enjoy their crafts, whether music or dancing. You find many of the same people travel from festival to festival; they all know each other and enjoy dancing or playing instruments together.

In the musical competitions, you'll find those competing against each other will also back each other up in their competitions. You may see one person compete in banjo and have a friend back up on the guitar, then those same two people swap instruments – competing against each other but also supporting each other. It's one of the rare competitions where people encourage one another in such a lovely way. Just as my father told me many years ago, **there will always be someone better than you**; *the trick to this is finding* *that person and learning from them.* Bluegrass Festivals embody this in a way I have never seen anywhere else.

Amelia learned much from that jam before her competition. She nervously waited and was ready.

Her number was called and she danced. She did a fantastic job. The clogging great who helped her at the jam came over and talked to her after her dance. Jason Wade told her how proud he was of her. Clogging is one of the neat events where just as many men as women compete.

When five names in her age category were announced to advance to the finals, Amelia's name was not called. You could see her face change as they called all five names and hers was missing from the list. The clogging great – Mr. Jason, as Amelia called him – came over and congratulated her on advancing to the finals. She had not advanced. He thought she had advanced to the finals to dance later in the evening. However, she didn't. She was disappointed but not crushed. She knew there were others better than her at the competition but she had fun. She had learned from those who were better. She learned in a way that made her better.

We packed up our chairs and passed by another jam session with a dancing board. We saw a man in his 70s with a head full of white hair, his pants legs pulled up and wearing different colored socks, to call attention to his feet. We stopped and let both girls dance. Jason Wade came up and told us how best to practice with Amelia when we got home. He is one of the people we can learn from; his wisdom on dancing was what we needed to help Amelia get better. *There is always someone better than you; the trick is to find them and learn from them.*

It took me a long time to learn this lesson. The lesson that my dad was trying to teach me so many years ago sitting on the front porch of our house when I was disappointed that I didn't get the first chair in the band. The lesson isn't that you can't be great. It's that there will always be someone who can teach you more about the craft you are working on, no matter what that art is in life. If you look close enough, there is always someone better and willing to help.

People who are truly great at their craft, no matter what that work is will share their wisdom with those who want to get better. They won't hold their knowledge to themselves. They want to pass it along. I now know that when others get better, we all get better.

Lesson 9

Say Goodbye Like You Say Hello

"You and I will meet again, when we're least expecting it, one day in some far off place, I will recognize your face, I won't say goodbye my friend, for you and I will meet again"
– Tom Petty

"DAD, I AM TAKING A NEW JOB," I said these words confidently to my dad, faking the confidence a little more than was necessary to ward off the feelings of butterflies in my stomach that I could not stop from flying around. I knew my dad would not approve of my news.

My dad, who never understood why I changed jobs so much just sighed and laughed, a sign I knew meant he did not approve and my overconfidence did not prevent him from feeling that way. At that point in my young career, I changed jobs every couple of years – professionally restless.

There were so many opportunities waiting, new people to meet, new skills to acquire and never enough time to explore them all. Plus, with each job change, I increased my salary, substantially.

"Donita, I'm going to have to get you a new Rolodex card in my file." The Rolodex in question sat on his desk in his office, where, at that point in time, he had worked for more than 30 years. It was a Rolodex on a wheel, which flipped 360 degrees to display the contacts. Dad liked having the numbers written on the old fashion Rolodex, rather than stored in an electronic filing system or in an address book. My dad, very practical in nature, always had a reason for everything he did.

He could touch the numbers on his Rolodex; he could rearrange them, alphabetize them as new contacts came and, of course, remove those that no longer needed to be there. Eventually, he gave up writing my numbers down and made me write it on the Rolodex card, so I would see how many times numbers had been crossed out and added to the simple card.

"What are you going to do?" he asked.

"I'm going to work for another healthcare company," I said.

For three years, I had been on assignment to a large healthcare company as a contract employee in information technology. My journey meandering through this company as a result of a few fortunate events made me realize that sometimes, good luck and answers to prayers were just as important as skills. I loved the company I was working for and wanted a permanent position to be paid on the same ledger as so many of the people I worked alongside, my work family. However, I just did not seem to have the skills needed to be hired as an employee.

"Say goodbye like you said hello," he told me. That piece of advice stuck. This job had been very good to me. For three years, I made many wonderful friends who would go on to be with me for many years. I had a boss who presented me so many opportunities and also understood that I needed to become a full-time employee with benefits like those most everyone else was receiving.

Contracted employees, like I was, did not get the same benefits as employees at this company since they were hired for a period of time. I also wanted to get my master's degree and needed the company's tuition reimbursement to assist.

"Dad, I'll give them 3 weeks' notice and you know that's great advice. I think I'll write everyone I work with a thank you note." And I did just that.

Always nervous when turning in my notice but also enjoying a little bit of the buzz that followed and conversations from curious people on why I was leaving. As a lover of people, I always enjoyed the conversations with them. Heeding the advice of my dad: *"Say goodbye like you said hello,"* I worked harder than ever during the weeks on notice. I often stayed late in the evening and worked well after 8:00 PM my last night there.

Being a trusted member of the team, I was instructed to leave my badge with the security officer at the front desk of our building and leave my laptop on my desk.

My last task before turning in my badge was hand delivering my written thank you notes. There were more than twenty I had written. I wrote letters to those who were paramount to my career: friends, mentors, and supervisors. Leaving that evening, I sat down on the curb and cried.

Not sure I had made the right decision, but knowing it was a decision that I had made and one that was final, or, at least, I thought it was.

The next week I was starting my new job. It was as if I knew that night crying on the curb that my decision to leave would haunt me but also know that I needed the opportunity to spread my wings.

The first week at my new job was one of misery. The new team was not welcoming. The office layout was terrible. The commute was more than I had anticipated. The company culture was not one that was conducive to working with others; it was combative and awkward. I did not fit them, and they did not fit my idea of a great place to work.

I called my boss from my previous job and told him of the grave mistake I had made. He asked me to speak to my new boss about my future both long term and short term with the company and to call him back with the answer, and he also said, "You need to make a lot of mistakes in life; that's how you learn."

The answer was pretty noncommittal from my new boss. He told me I would be answering his phone and opening his mail...this was not the exciting job I had anticipated.

I left a job where I was managing a fifty million dollar budget, auditing telecom invoices and finding millions of dollars that were paid in error, saving the company I had worked for more money than I had ever thought possible.

Answering the phone? Opening mail? That sounded like a cushy job, and I would wither and die in a situation like that. I could not imagine a job without a lot of demands and pressure. What had I done?

I called my previous boss back and relayed the information. He told me to call again the next day. He had an idea and needed a few hours to get something in the works. Thankfully, the next day he had a great solution, and I was afforded the opportunity to come back to my old job at twice the salary I was making when I left.

When I arrived at my old job, my boss handed me the thank you note that I had left for him and said, "I don't need this anymore; you can have it back." Saying goodbye like you said hello gave me the opportunity to radically change my life and set my career on a trajectory that would have never been possible had I not said goodbye better than I had said hello to that group. I left my team in a better place than they were before I arrived and cared about them so much in the last weeks of my notice that it hurt to leave them.

I left that company one other time, for six years, and returned again. An opportunity many people do not get. The second time I left, I followed the same model and worked diligently until the end, except for this time I stayed the last night until almost midnight. Working on a large contract and providing my feedback. Driving home that evening, I knew I had made the right decision this time, and it was time to move on to a new opportunity. How I said goodbye both times gave me the chance to return a third time to this company and realize that third time is a charm. This was a far cry from the first time I left a professional job.

I had many jobs growing up and often worked two or three jobs at the same time during the summer as a way to pay my way through college. One summer, I worked waiting tables at the local Ponderosa Steakhouse, worked at an ice cream store and worked at Radio Shack.

My first job out of school was working at a travel agency full time. This was before the days of the internet when travel agents were valued and their advice highly coveted by travelers. This was a time when airline tickets were actual tickets.

I worked in this travel agency during college and took the opportunity to take a full-time position with them when I graduated from Austin Peay State University with an Accounting Degree. The travel agency's office was small, typically with only two to three employees and we provided services to both businesses and individuals. It was a fun job, and I enjoyed the interaction with the people and the work itself. However, I also knew that long term, I needed more growth opportunity. During my first full-time year at the travel agency, the airlines started capping the sales commission travel agents were paid and the industry seemed to be going in a way that was not positive for the small town agencies.

I looked around for another job and secured a position with a start-up company and as a result, started my lifelong pursuit of a career in information technology. I would be making more money than at the travel agency, in this new job, and knew it was the right thing to do for my career, but leaving was not something that excited me. It left me with a sick feeling in my gut and being a recent college graduate and also a recent newlywed, I was facing life challenges that I was neither familiar with nor had the maturity to handle.

In fact, I handled the departure from the travel agency terribly. My actions still leave me embarrassed. I resigned from the company giving them two weeks to find another person to fill my shoes. I had personally paid for a membership to a travel service for travel agents that provided me with discounts for vacations, hotels, and car rentals. After I left, the owner of the agency asked me to return the card for this travel service. Since I had personally paid for this card, I did not feel the need to hand it over and I ignored her request. A second request came, followed by a third. I was outraged that she would want this back – the principle of it was just not worth it on either side. However, not making the right decision, I cut the card up and mailed it to her, a hot-headed choice that 20 years later still haunts me.

This past week I traveled more than 200 miles to visit with an employee who had turned in his notice. We threw the employee a party, lunch of nachos and laughs. After the party, I sat down and talked to the employee to make sure that he was comfortable with his decision. Once I knew he was, I told him that we wanted to *say goodbye like we said hello* to him, actually even better. I also said that we would be glad to have him back if the need ever arose. He just needed to call me if that happened. He left, shook my hand and thanked me for the lunch and the advice.

There are many opportunities to *say goodbye like you say hello* and not all of them are in jobs.

Acknowledgments

Every good book has an acknowledgment section. Just as every good author has a set of champions, who help the author create their story and publish. My story is no different.

First, thank you to my husband, Robert. Robert, your support is and always has been unwavering. You never doubt me and still support my crazy dreams. Thank you. You are a great husband and father.

Second, thank you to my daughters, Amelia and Reagan. You make me proud. I hope that as you continue to blossom, you find wise people and listen.

Third, thank you to my sisters, Danielle and Deidre. Danielle, thank you for always telling me you are proud of me. I am proud of you. You are my best friend and my cheerleader. Deidre, thank you for always wanting to know what I'm doing. I am proud of you.

Thank you to my book coach, Deb and the incredible team at Author Accelerator without your coaching and guidance, this book would still be an outline.

Thank you to my early readers. Julie, Jim, Andre, Andrew, Sarah, and Barbara. Your feedback was paramount to this becoming a reality.

Last but indeed, not least, thank you to my Dad, Kenneth Taylor. Thank you for sharing your outlook on life with me. Most importantly, thank you for your wisdom.

DONITA M. BROWN

Epilogue

While writing this book, I realized how important the people in my life are; how each person in my life has planted a seed of wisdom. Enclosed in the book, you have already found a stamped thank you note. I would love for you to send one to someone who has given you advice that has shaped your life. Take a picture and post it to your social media app of preference and tag it with #WisdomFromOthers to share it with me. You can also connect with me on Twitter or Instagram. I'm listed as @DonitaBrown.

Will you start a movement with me?

ABOUT THE AUTHOR

Donita is a listener.

She listens to others and has spent much of her life
learning and reading.

She has been married to the love of her life for 18
years.

Donita and Robert are blessed with two beautiful and active daughters, Amelia and Reagan and their standard poodle, named Chief. Donita lives in Springfield, TN with her family and loves to hike and be outdoors.

Donita Brown a Director for Hospital Corporation of America (HCA), based in Nashville, TN. A seasoned executive, Donita has served in several leadership positions for HCA.

Donita is an adjunct professor at the Jack C. Massey School of Business MBA Program for Belmont University and for Lipscomb University, teaching classes at both the School of Business and Masters level. She is a distinguished graduate of the HCA Infrastructure Technology and Services, Emerging Leader Program.

Donita holds an MBA from Belmont University and a Bachelor of Business Administration in Accounting Degree from Austin Peay State University. She is currently working towards completion of a doctorate degree in Business.